NORTH EAST
STEAM
1948-1968

PETER TUFFREY

GREAT NORTHERN

ACKNOWLEDGEMENTS

I am grateful for help received from the following people: Roger Arnold, David Burrill, John Chalcraft, Paul Chancellor, David Christie, D.J. Dippie, John Law, Michael Mercer, Hugh Parkin, Bill Reed, Andrew, Rachel and Sue Warnes, Tony Watson, Bill Wright.

Gratitude should also be expressed to my son Tristram for his general help and encouragement throughout the course of the project.

Great Northern Books
PO Box 1380, Bradford, BD5 5FB
www.greatnorthernbooks.co.uk

ISBN: 978-1-914227-24-0

Design and layout: David Burrill

CIP Data
A catalogue for this book is available from the British Library

INTRODUCTION

The year 2022 marks 55 years since the demise of steam on the main lines in North East England. This event was not only the end of an era, but a major point in the decline of the area's great industries – coal mining, shipbuilding and steel production. All had risen to prosperity together in the mid-19th century and collapsed within thirty years of each other at the end of the 20th century.

North East England consists of over 3,000 square miles of land grouped into three counties: Durham; Northumberland; Tyne and Wear. There are three cities – Newcastle, Durham and Sunderland – as well as several towns: Middlesbrough, Gateshead, Darlington, Hartlepool and Stockton-on-Tees.

Importantly, the area sits over the 'Great Northern' coalfield. The measures were exploited from the 17th century and demand for the resource also came from other areas of Britain, as well as abroad. This induced colliery owners to develop means of transport. Wagonways were devised to take the coal to the River Tyne where ships carried off the minerals. Limitations of wooden rails, capacity of horses and the slow transport times spurred further innovations. At Killingworth Colliery, George Stephenson was inspired to work on steam technology. He later became involved with the Hetton Colliery Railway which was designed and built to use cast iron rails, stationary steam engines and steam locomotives.

The Stockton & Darlington Railway approached Stephenson as a result of his experience and he became instrumental in the project. On opening in September 1825, the line became the first public railway to use steam locomotives. As coal was 'king' – and went on to be for the next 150 years – there was little thought at the time for transporting passengers. Initially, the S&DR left this activity for others, before taking the role upon themselves.

A competitor to the Stockton & Darlington company was the Clarence Railway. The line was promoted to connect County Durham with Stockton and the River Tees. Operations began in 1833 for coal traffic and from 1835 horse-drawn passenger services were offered. This route later extended northward to Sunderland along the coast.

The Stanhope & Tyne Railway was developed to transport limestone and coal to South Shields and ran trains from September 1834, being reluctant to engage in passenger service. Public demand soon saw this change, as in mid-April 1835 the conveyance of people began, though at first on top of the coal before a dedicated wagon was provided. As the railways in the area developed, improved connections were deemed desirable and a deviation from the original route from the south (Darlington and Durham) to Gateshead and Newcastle was made in 1850. The line was the main East Coast route until diverted via Durham in the early 1870s.

Following the establishment of these local mineral and freight lines, thoughts turned to connecting to the wider area. The Great North of England Railway joined York with Darlington in 1841 and from there transport links with much of Southern England were available. At this time passengers could reach Newcastle also, yet by using several railways to reach the city. The GNER was authorised to continue on to Newcastle but the company ran out of funds before the line could progress. The Newcastle Junction Railway was surveyed to bridge the gap using the existing mineral lines, such as the Pontop & South Shields Railway and Brandling Junction Railway. The route was authorised in 1842 and completed two years later, with the journey time to London around twelve hours. With this finished, the task of reaching Edinburgh was tackled by the Newcastle & Berwick Railway and North British Railway.

As many of the main lines were completed by the early 1850s, the individual companies decided to consolidate their power. The North Eastern Railway was formed in 1854, mainly from the York & North Midland, York, Newcastle & Berwick and Leeds Northern Railways, in addition to some smaller concerns, whilst a number of lines were subsequently taken over. The NER was not averse to joining with other major companies to operate joint lines and stations, with these mainly in Yorkshire. The NER dominated the North East and only the NBR made any kind of encroachment into the area, with lines to Hexham and Morpeth. Before the First World War, the NER had 1,700 route miles, 500 stations, carried over 60,000,000 passengers and had receipts of over £11,300,000. After costs, the company made approx. £4,000,000.

In the late 19th and early 20th centuries, the locomotive affairs of the NER were overseen by Wilson Worsdell and then Sir Vincent Raven. Both mainly produced designs for mineral/freight engines which numbered several dozen and went on to be the backbone of the fleet in the North East to the end of steam. Worsdell concentrated on the 0-6-0 tender engine for the traffic requirements and 320 were built over four variations (P to P3) between 1894 and 1909. He also added 90 0-8-0 tender locomotives (T and T1), with the wheel arrangement being favoured by Raven who ordered 120 T2s (LNER Class Q6) from Darlington. A small number of P3s were also added by Raven, though a significant number of E1 0-6-0Ts (LNER J72) were built to Worsdell's design and tripled the total in traffic. An important Raven design was the S3 4-6-0 (LNER B16) which utilised three cylinders and had a role working both freight and passenger trains.

The London & North Eastern Railway inherited the NER's territory at the Grouping of 1923. Over 2,000 locomotives also passed into the hands of the new company. As mentioned, many were recently-built freight locomotives, yet the company's passenger locomotives were not particularly strong and soon Gresley's A1 Pacifics (later A3) took the reins on the principal expresses. In the late

1920s and early 1930s, the D49 4-4-0 began to work the secondary expresses in the area. A premier service between Newcastle and King's Cross began in 1935 utilising Gresley's streamlined A4 Class Pacific. This class went on to grow for general service and became a fixture on the East Coast Main Line. Speed was a feature of railway promotion in the late 1930s and for freight traffic the V2 Class 2-6-2 was introduced, also taking a role on passenger trains. For local services, the North East was provided with the V1/V3 Class 2-6-2T. During the Second World War, the motive power was tested by the demands of the war effort and reinforcements were deployed in the form of War Department 'Austerity' 2-8-0s and later by WD 0-6-0ST locomotives for shunting duties. The LNER provided several new designs just before Nationalisation: Thompson A2/3 and Peppercorn A1 Class Pacifics; Thompson B1 Class 4-6-0s; Peppercorn K1 Class 2-6-0s.

The railways were officially Nationalised by the Labour Government in 1948 and the LNER was split into three regions, with one comprising the North East. Whilst other areas received significant numbers of British Railways Standard Class locomotives, the North Eastern Region did not and the major representation consisted of 9F Class 2-10-0s. These were used on the Consett to Tyne Dock iron ore service, in partnership with specially-constructed hopper wagons. These had side discharge and the locomotives were fitted with Westinghouse air pumps to operate the doors. Another new design to see use in the area was H.G. Ivatt's 4MT 2-6-0, which was originally produced for the London Midland & Scottish Railway but deemed suitable for use elsewhere.

In addition to the mainline fleet, the National Coal Board employed a large number of shunting locomotives for moving coal and wagons around the various North East complexes. The Lambton Railway was originally a self-contained system before Nationalisation and continued subsequently. The Earls of Durham – the Lambton family – had drawn on the riches present in their land by sinking several pits to reach the coal measures in the area. Steam first ran on the Lambton Railway in 1814 and the concern subsequently grew to 70 miles of lines with access to Sunderland Docks. At the height of the Lambton Colliery Co. several dozen locomotives were at work and dedicated repair shops were established at Philadelphia. Similarly, the Blyth & Tyne Railway gradually expanded from early wooden wagonways feeding coal from the pits to the Tyne to a larger operation connecting much of the area from the Tyne to the Wansbeck rivers. In the late 1850s, the route was extended from Bedlington to Morpeth and shortly afterwards went from Bedlington to North Seaton. Ashington and Newbiggin-by-the-Sea joined the network in the early 1870s.

North East Steam explores the aforementioned areas and locomotives, using over 200 superb black-and-white and colour images to document the rich railway scene of the area. The highly-evocative photographs have been captured by several well-known photographers at stations, sheds, workshops and the lineside. With the North East now much changed, the book offers a timely reminder of the illustrious heritage of the area.

Peter Tuffrey
Doncaster, May 2022

Above ALNMOUTH – NO. 60836
Light engine at Alnmouth on 12th May 1966 is Gresley V2 Class 2-6-2 no. 60836. At the start of the year 14 class members were still in service, though at the end of the year all had been condemned. No. 60836 went in December from Dundee. Photograph courtesy Rail-Online.

Below ALNMOUTH – NO. 64916
Gresley J39 Class 0-6-0 no. 64916 stands at Alnmouth station with a local train, c. 1960. The locomotive arrived at the local shed in mid-1955 and worked there to withdrawal in August 1961. Photograph by P. Moffat courtesy Colour-Rail.

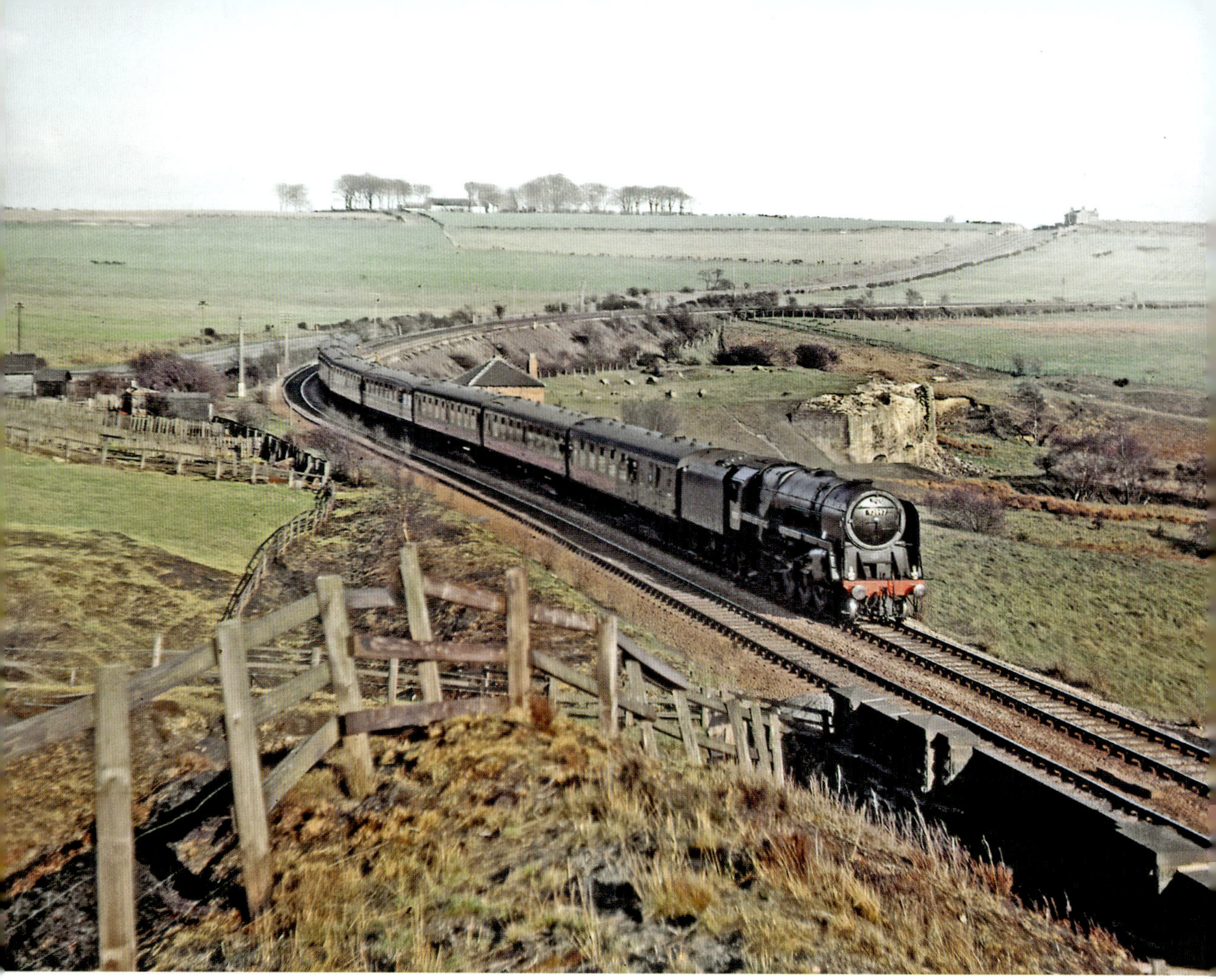

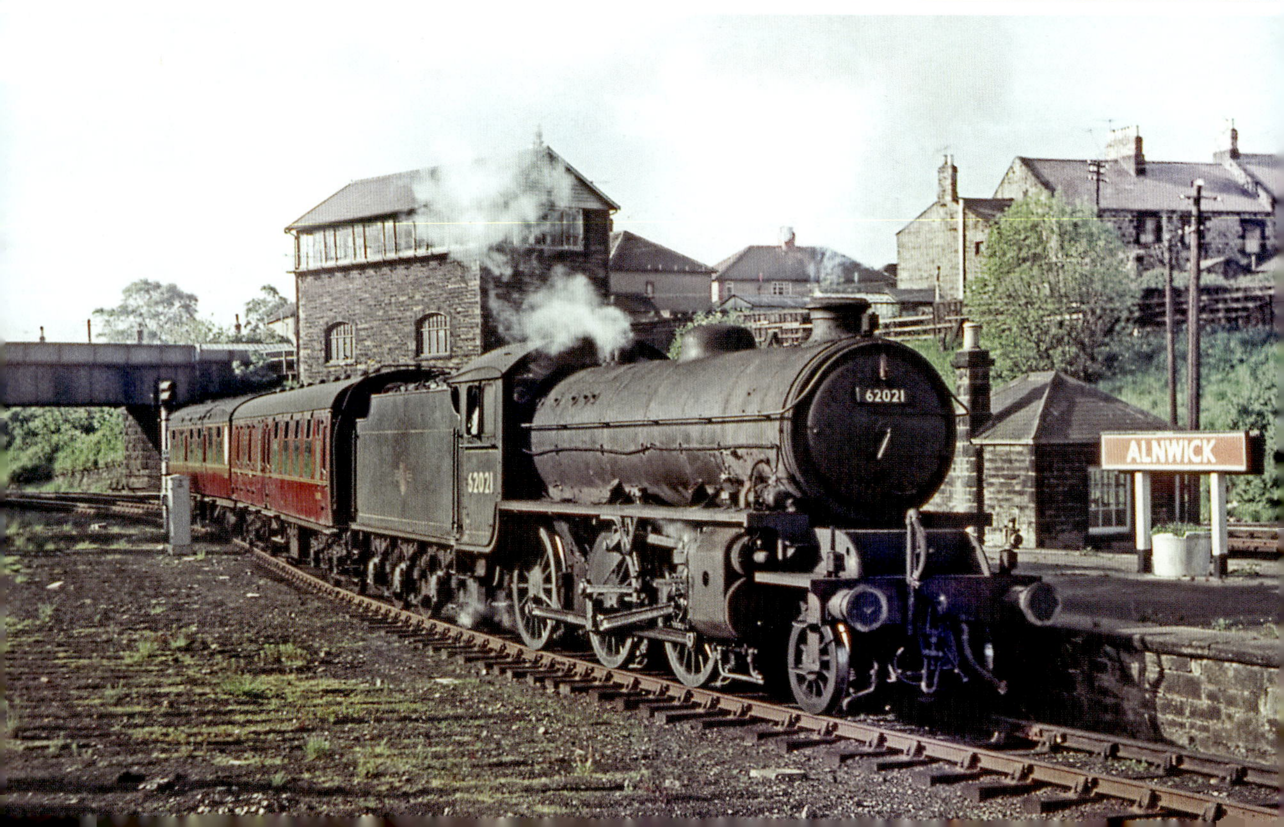
62021
ALNWICK
62021

Above ASHINGTON COLLIERY, HIRST PLATFORM – NO. 43137

The Ashington Colliery Company offered trains to transport both employees and local people around the area. Several platforms existed though the main departure point was Hirst platform near Ashington Colliery. Services were provided from the 1880s on a narrow-gauge line before a standard gauge system was laid at the turn of the century. A high number of trains were still offered in the mid-1960s before closure in 1966. Passing Hirst platform with a loaded coal train in 1967 is Ivatt Class 4MT 2-6-0 no. 43137. The locomotive was employed nearby at Blyth and was condemned in September 1967. Photograph courtesy Rail-Online.

Opposite above ANNFIELD PLAIN – NO. 92097

Between Consett and Stanley at Annfield Plain, BR Standard Class 9F 2-10-0 no. 92097 has the Railway Correspondence & Travel Society's 'North Eastern No. 2' railtour on 10th April 1964. This began the day at Leeds with preserved Gresley K4 Class 2-6-0 no. 3442 *The Great Marquess* and travelled northward to Newcastle. There, no. 92097 took over and delivered the group to Consett where a DMU transported them forward on the Stanhope & Tyne Railway mineral branch to Waskerley and back. No. 92097 returned to the train and deposited the tour at Darlington for no. 3442 to complete the day to Leeds. Photograph by Chris Davies courtesy Rail Photoprints.

Opposite below ALNWICK STATION – NO. 62021

The 07.50 train from Alnmouth has deposited passengers at Alnwick station on 2nd June 1966 and is now reversing away. The station was opened in 1850 at the end of a three-mile branch from the main line at Alnmouth. Rebuilt by the North Eastern Railway in 1887, Alnwick was in use until 1968 and the line was later lifted. The Aln Valley Railway was formed in the mid-1990s with plans to reopen the branch and has been successful to present, operating around a mile of line. Photograph by Hugh Ballantyne courtesy Rail Photoprints.

Below **ASHINGTON COLLIERY – NO. 6**
Ashington Colliery opened in the late 1860s and in the 1890s gave the name to the company operating several pits in the area. The colliery's peak employment was reached in the 1920s when over 5,000 pairs of hands toiled to win coal. At Nationalisation, Ashington produced approximately 1,000,000 tons. Output continued to the late 1980s. Peckett & Sons 0-6-0ST (works no. 2023) Ashington no. 6 has a train of steel hopper wagons at Ashington in August 1966. Photograph by A.J.B. Dodd courtesy Rail Photoprints.

Above **ASHINGTON COLLIERY – NO. 43123**

Introduced as a replacement for the many older 0-6-0s running on the London Midland & Scottish Railway in the late 1930s and 1940s, the Ivatt Class 4MT 2-6-0 went on to serve a similar role in other areas of the country. The first locomotive built to the design emerged into traffic during late 1947 and the production total eventually reached 162 when concluded in 1952. No. 43123 was one of seventy-five constructed as Horwich Works and completed there in August 1951. New to the North Eastern Region at Selby, the locomotive moved several times subsequently and was at North Blyth from November 1966 to July 1967. No. 43123 was one of several 4MTs that ended their careers at the depot towards the end of steam. The engine is pictured at Ashington Colliery with a loaded train of coal hoppers in 1964 when working from West Hartlepool. Photograph courtesy Rail Photoprints.

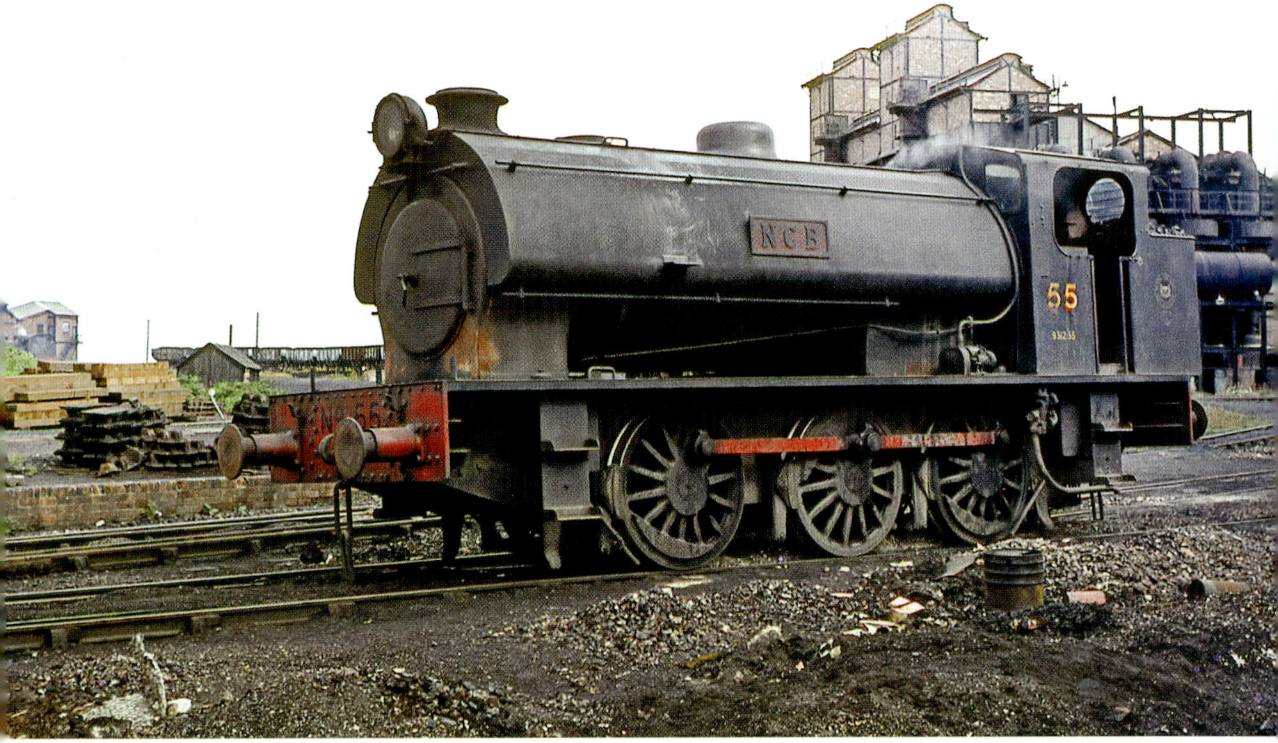
NCB
55

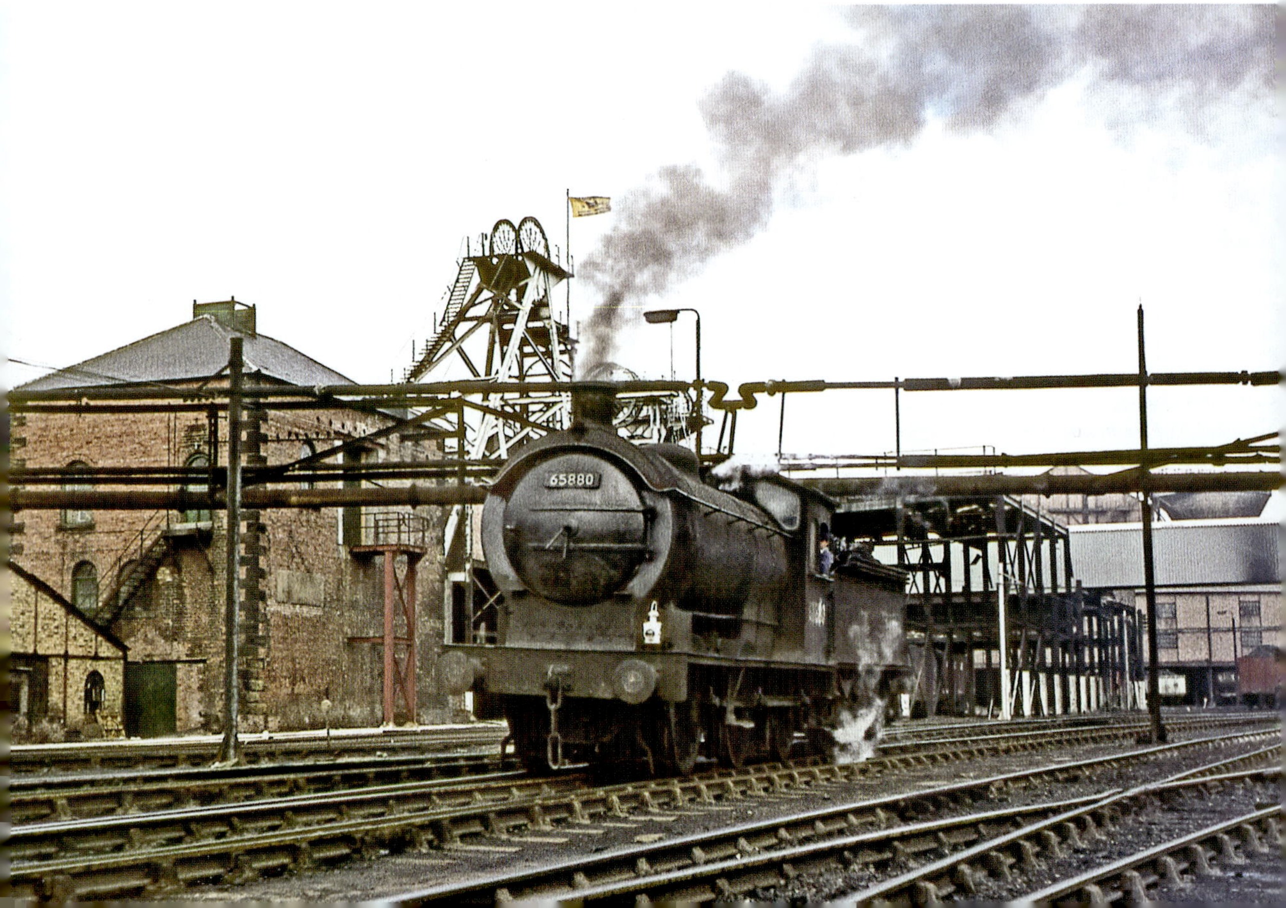
65880

Above **BILLINGHAM STATION – NO. 90434**
Following construction for the War Department, 'Austerity' 2-8-0 no. 90434 was taken into stock by the LNER as Class O7 no. 3113 at Hull Springhead shed. The engine subsequently remained in the North Eastern Area to withdrawal in June 1967. Seen at Billingham station with coal wagons on 12th April 1966, the locomotive was employed at West Hartlepool. Photograph by Geoff Warnes.

Opposite above **ASHINGTON COLLIERY – NO. 55**
When the War Department required a shunting locomotive early in the Second World War, the Hunslet Engine Co. suggested one of their own designs. This 0-6-0ST was accepted, becoming the 'Austerity' Class shunter, of which 377 were built for the War Department. As part of the 'war effort', several other manufacturers built the design, including Vulcan Foundry, which produced NCB no. 55 in 1945 (works no. 5279). In addition to surplus engines being taken over, the NCB ordered locomotives separately and over 70 were delivered to the mid-1960s. No. 55 is at Ashington Colliery in August 1965. Photograph by A.J.B. Dodd courtesy Rail Photoprints.

Opposite below **ASHINGTON COLLIERY – NO. 65880**
In the yard at Ashington Colliery during August 1966 is Worsdell J27 Class no. 65880. Built at Darlington in August 1922, the locomotive was in service to June 1967. North Blyth shed mainly employed the engine under BR, though the last six months passed at Sunderland depot. Photograph by A.J.B. Dodd courtesy Rail Photoprints.

Below BILLINGHAM STATION – NO. 62007

As a competitor to the Stockton & Darlington Railway, the Clarence Railway was promoted to connect County Durham with Stockton and the River Tees. Operations began in 1833 for coal traffic and from 1835 horse-drawn passenger services were offered. A point of collection was provided at Billingham, though a station was not built until 1841 when the Stockton & Hartlepool extended the line from Billingham to docks at Hartlepool. This route later extended northward to Sunderland along the coast. On 12th April 1966, Billingham station had just six months left before being closed and resited, with the buildings depicted here demolished. Peppercorn K1 no. 62007 has a northbound train of coal wagons. Photograph by Geoff Warnes.

Above BISHOP AUCKLAND STATION – NO. 42405

The Stockton & Darlington Railway extended their line to Bishop Auckland in 1843. Subsequently, several other routes radiated from the town, including those to Barnard Castle and beyond, Wearhead, Consett, Durham and Brancepeth. As these lines were built, Bishop Auckland station was required to change, the first occurring in 1857, then 1867 and lastly during 1905 when made a triangular junction. Approaching from the east under Newgate Street bridge in the early 1960s is Fowler 4P Class 2-6-4T no. 42405. The engine transferred into the North Eastern Region from Mirfield to Sowerby Bridge, which was originally in the London Midland Region before boundary changes, in early 1958 and reached Darlington in 1962 for the final two years in traffic. In the 1980s the station was realigned. Photograph courtesy Rail-Online.

Opposite above BOLDON COLLIERY – NO. 65835

On 22nd July 1961, a mid-afternoon freight is at Boldon Colliery with Worsdell J27 Class 0-6-0 no. 65835. The locomotive was constructed by Robert Stephenson & Hawthorns Ltd in July 1909 and was in service until January 1967. When pictured, no. 65835 was employed at Thornaby and transferred to North Blyth before condemned. Photograph by D.J. Dippie.

Opposite below BLAYDON – NO. 65890

West of Gateshead at Blaydon, Worsdell J27 Class 0-6-0 no. 65890 passes with a train of coal empties on 25th September 1962. The design was introduced by the North Eastern Railway in 1906 as the P3 Class and construction continued to 1923. No. 65890 was amongst the final batch of ten built at Darlington Works in summer 1923 and this group was equipped with a superheater from new. The preceding 25 P3s were also fitted, whilst the other class members were subsequently given an improved boiler. No. 65890 was in traffic to May 1963. Photograph courtesy Rail Photoprints.

Below BISHOP AUCKLAND STATION – NO. 61037

Spanning several days, the 'North Eastern Tour' of late September/early October 1963 visited a number of places of interest in the area. Thompson B1 no. 61037 *Jairou* was used on 28th September for the Bishop Auckland to St John's Chapel portion and is at the aforementioned, viewed from Newgate Street bridge. Photograph by T.B. Owen courtesy Colour-Rail.

BOLDON COLLIERY – NO. 65666
With brake van at Boldon Colliery on 1st
March 1960 is Worsdell J25 Class 0-6-0 no.
65666. The engine was withdrawn in July.
Photograph by D.J. Dippie.

Above BLAYDON SHED – NO. 63356
Raven Q6 0-8-0 no. 63356 was a long-term resident at Blaydon shed, this lasting 15 years. In the yard on 24th May 1961, the locomotive moved on to North Blyth in September 1962. A Gresley A3 is seen in the background. Photograph by D.J. Dippie.

Below BOLDON COLLIERY STATION – NO. 63760
Originally belonging to J.G. Robinson's O4 Class design, no. 63760 was reconstructed to Edward Thompson's O1 specifications in August 1946. The locomotive has a train of coal wagons at Boldon Colliery station on 1st March 1960. Photograph by D.J. Dippie.

Above **BOLDON COLLIERY STATION – NO. 62060**
In the mid-1860s, coal production began at Boldon, north of Sunderland. Brockley Whins station was initially provided to serve the area, yet this later became Boldon Colliery in March 1926. Peppercorn K1 no. 62060 passes through there with a coal train for Tyne Dock during 1967. Photograph by John Atkinson courtesy Rail-Online.

Below **BOWES RAILWAY – NO. 6 AND NO. 19**
Coal from Springwell (between Gateshead and Washington) was transported to the Tyne at Jarrow on the Bowes Railway. Two locomotives employed on the line were 0-6-0ST no. 6 and 0-4-0ST no. 19 and are seen on 15th September 1962. Photograph by John Briggs courtesy A1 Steam Trust.

Above BRANCEPETH STATION – NO. 67248

On the line between Durham and Bishop Auckland, Brancepeth station opened under the North Eastern Railway in April 1857. Worsdell G5 Class 0-4-4T no. 67248 has a southbound train there in April 1957. Closure occurred in 1964. Photograph courtesy Rail-Online.

Below BURNMOOR – NO. 52

Former Taff Valley Railway 0-6-2T locomotive Lambton no. 52 is shunting at Burnmoor on 20th September 1965. The Great Western Railway sold the engine to Lambton Collieries in the 1930s. Photograph by Hugh Ballantyne courtesy Rail Photoprints.

CASTLE EDEN VIADUCT

North of Hartlepool on the coast line, a Peppercorn K1 (no. 6204X) crosses Castle Eden viaduct, also known as Horden viaduct, with a northbound train during 1967. Photograph courtesy Rail-Online.

Above **COATHAM MUNDEVILLE – NO. 60877**
Between Darlington and Newton Aycliffe on the East Coast Main Line, Gresley V2 Class no. 60877 has a partially fitted express freight at Coatham Mundeville on 9th July 1963. Photograph by D.J. Dippie.

Below **COCKFIELD FELL STATION – NO. 69875**
A local train is with Raven A8 Class 4-6-2T no. 69875 at Cockfield Fell station during April 1957. The station was to close for passengers in the following year after nine decades serving the local community, though freight traffic lingered to 1962. Photograph courtesy Rail-Online.

CONSETT – NO. 63357 AND NO. 63439

A pair of Raven Q6 Class 0F8-0s is at Consett on 28th September 1963. They are no.63357 and no. 63439. Photograph by T.B. Owen courtesy Colour-Rail.

Above CONSETT – NO. 92064

The iron ore traffic between Tyne Dock and Consett was provided with special 56-ton capacity wagons mounted on two four-wheel bogies, with side discharge. In the early 1950s thirty were built at Shildon. BR Standard Class 9F 2-10-0 no. 92064 has a train of the wagons at Consett in the 1960s. Photograph by Joe Richardson courtesy Colour-Rail.

Below CORBRIDGE STATION – NO. 65103

A feature of many stations across the country was a floral display maintained by the staff. This was particularly the case for rural stations and a tour of those between Newcastle-Hexham-Morpeth was organised on 14th August 1955. Worsdell J21 Class 0-6-0 no. 65103 has the train at Corbridge station (east of Hexham) here. Photograph from the Dave Cobbe Collection courtesy Rail Photoprints.

CONSETT – NO. 92099

Loaded coal hoppers for Consett Steel Works pass Consett station behind 9F no. 92099 in July 1966. Photograph from the Dave Cobbe Collection courtesy Rail Photoprints.

Above DARLINGTON STATION – NO. 60009

As a promotional venture for the 'Zoom' lolly, Lyons Maid Ice Cream organised several rail tours in the summer of 1964. One involved Gresley A4 no. 60009 *Union of South Africa* travelling from Edinburgh Waverley to York and return. A stop has been made at Darlington here. Photograph by John Arnott-Brown courtesy A1 Steam Trust.

Below CROOK STATION – NO. 69851

Crook station was opened as the Stockton & Darlington Railway extended westward to Bishop Auckland and Crook in the 1840s. Later, the line advanced onward to Tow Law and Waskerley. A local train from Tow Law to Darlington is at Crook in November 1955 with Raven A8 Class 4-6-2T no. 69851. Photograph courtesy Rail-Online.

Above DARLINGTON SHED – NO. 60124
The mainline standby engine was often left to simmer in sidings at Darlington shed towards the end of steam. Peppercorn A1 Class Pacific no. 60124 *Kenilworth* has the assignment on 3rd January 1966. Just under two months in service remained for the locomotive. Photograph by Neil Simpson courtesy A1 Steam Trust.

Below DARLINGTON STATION – NO. 60118
A1 no. 60118 *Archibald Sturrock* pauses at Darlington station in 1964. Photograph by Michael Denholm courtesy A1 Steam Trust.

Above DARLINGTON SHED – NO. 61757
Gresley K2 Class 2-6-0 no. 61757 was withdrawn from Boston in early 1959 and has reached Darlington shed for storage before being scrapped at the works. Photograph by Bill Reed.

Below DARLINGTON SHED – NO. 60004
Darlington Works continued to accept steam repairs for several years after Doncaster ceased offering the service. Gresley A4 no. 60004 *William Whitelaw* has travelled from Aberdeen for attention in late June 1965 and is at Darlington shed before entering the shops. Photograph by Bill Reed.

Above DARLINGTON STATION – NO. 61463

At the end of the First World War, Sir Vincent Raven designed a new mixed traffic 4-6-0 with three cylinders. This was the NER S3 Class, LNER B16, which went on to number 70 examples constructed at Darlington between 1919 and 1924. No. 61463 was a late addition to stock in November 1923. Under Sir Nigel Gresley, several of the class were rebuilt with outside Walschaerts valve gear and his '2 to 1' lever operating the valves for the middle cylinder in place of the original Stephenson motion for all cylinders. Edward Thompson rebuilt a total of 17 with separate valve gear operating the three cylinders, including no. 61463 in November 1947. The locomotive has an express freight train at Darlington station on 15th October 1958. York-allocated, no. 61463 had 18 months in Hull before withdrawn in June 1964. Photograph by D.J. Dippie.

Opposite DARLINGTON STATION – NO. 60084

In the early 20th century, the North Eastern Railway and North British Railway joined forces to offer a train from Leeds to Edinburgh via York and Newcastle which was timed to allow further connections northward to Aberdeen and Perth, as well as to Glasgow. This train, and the return, survived Grouping and Nationalisation, at which time the name the 'North Briton' was bestowed upon the service. In the 1950s, the schedule was a 09.05 departure from Leeds with 35 minutes allowed to York and Darlington was reached at 10.27. Arrival in Edinburgh was set at 13.32 and on to Glasgow in another 85 minutes. The return left at 16.01 and was due at Leeds for 22.02. The northbound train is at Darlington station on 13th October 1958 with Gresley A3 Pacific no. 60084 *Trigo* leading the coaches. The locomotive was built as an A3 in February 1930 and was based in the North East at Gateshead and Heaton to September 1949 when a transfer to Leeds Neville Hill occurred. For the last year in traffic no. 60084 returned to Gateshead and was later scrapped at Hughes Bolckow, North Blyth. Photograph by D.J. Dippie.

Above DARLINGTON SHED – NO. 60124

Just north of Darlington station, the NER built a roundhouse on the eastern side of the main line in 1866 and this remained standing in use until the end of steam on the site 100 years later. A second through-road building was constructed in the mid-1880s, though this was rebuilt by the LNER just before the Second World War and the number of lines was reduced from nine to seven. Standing outside the new building on 2nd June 1965 is a particularly well-presented Peppercorn A1 Pacific, no. 60124 *Kenilworth*. Six months earlier the locomotive arrived at Darlington from York. Photograph by Chris Davies courtesy Rail Photoprints.

Opposite above DARLINGTON STATION – NO. 60134

The next generation of East Coast Main Line express engine was produced by A.H. Peppercorn just before the demise of the LNER at the end of 1947. The first of these A1 Class Pacifics appeared from Doncaster in August 1948 and 49 were constructed, with Darlington contributing 23 of the total. No. 60134 *Foxhunter* was the product of the latter in November 1948 and found employment in the Leeds area (latterly at Neville Hill) through to withdrawal in October 1965. The engine is close to this date here, as a relief express is at Darlington station with no. 60134 on 28th August and bound for Newcastle. In a particularly deplorable condition, the nameplates have been removed, scorching has occurred to the smokebox door and the top and bottom-right electric lights are broken or missing. Photograph by Chris Davies courtesy Rail Photoprints.

Opposite below DARLINGTON SHED – NO. 92098

Darlington was the designated workshop for heavy repairs carried out on the BR Standard Class 9F. Light attention was provided at both Stratford and Gateshead, whilst Doncaster did allow entry to the class on at least two occasions. BR hoped that intermediate repairs (no boiler lift) were to be carried out after 100,000 miles and a general repair following 200,000. No. 92098's first intermediate occurred in mid-1959 after three years in traffic at 75% of the allotted figure whilst the general took place in early 1962 at nearly 140,000 miles. The engine's last visit to Darlington Works was in August 1964 and this lasted to the end of October. No. 92098 is at the shed after the work was completed and ready to resume employment at Tyne Dock shed which lasted to July 1966 when sent for scrap. Photograph by John Arnott-Brown courtesy A1 Steam Trust.

Above DARLINGTON NORTH ROAD STATION – NO. 82029

The site of the original Stockton & Darlington Railway station at Darlington was at North Road. The facility was rebuilt in 1842 in time for the opening of the westward extensions and again later in the century. Renaming to Darlington North Road occurred in October 1868, whilst the main line station became Bank Top, though open from 1842 as Darlington. The latter became the focal point for services and was substantially rebuilt, opening in 1887. BR Standard Class 2 2-6-2T no. 82029 has a local train at North Road on 25th August 1956. Photograph courtesy Rail-Online.

Below DARLINGTON NORTH ROAD STATION – NO. 60891

On 29th October 1959, Gresley V2 no. 60891 was officially ex-works following a general repair. The engine is at North Road station on the day and being run-in. Photograph by D.J. Dippie.

Above DARLINGTON WORKS SCRAPYARD – NO. 68045

The NER scrapped locomotives at several sites before Darlington Works established an area dedicated to the process under the LNER in the early 1930s. This was on land which ran adjacent to Hopetown Lane's eastern side near North Road station. The yard was kept busy with a variety of locomotives arriving from other areas to be disposed of, as well as 'foreign' lines under BR. At work in the yard on 10th September 1960 is ex-War Department 0-6-0ST, LNER J94 Class, no. 68045. Class mate no. 68039 was the final locomotive scrapped in the yard when closed during early 1964, though some engines were later disposed of on the works site. Photograph by D.J. Dippie.

Below DARLINGTON WORKS SCRAPYARD – NO. 62738

A pair of Gresley D49s is at Darlington to be scrapped on 26th October 1959. Rotary cam-fitted no. 62738 *The Zetland* is in front of piston valve no. 62707 *Lancashire*. Photograph by D.J. Dippie.

DARLINGTON WORKS SCRAPYARD — NO. 61440
Raven B16 Class 4-6-0 no. 61440. J94 Class 0-6-0ST no. 68072
and Worsdell J26 Class 0-6-0 no. 65577 are identifiable on the
scrap line at Darlington on 22nd October 1960. Photograph by
D.J. Dippie.

Above DARLINGTON WORKS SCRAPYARD – NO. 68676
A particularly distressing scene captured at Darlington Works scrapyard shows Worsdell J72 Class 0-6-0T no. 68676 around half-way through the dismantling process on 22nd October 1960. The engine had been nearly six weeks out of traffic. Photograph by D.J. Dippie.

Below DARLINGTON WORKS – NO. 67601
Inside Darlington Works on 22nd October 1960, Gresley V1 2-6-2T no. 67601 is undergoing repairs which would see the locomotive in service for a further 14 months. No. 67601 was scrapped at Darlington by late 1962. Photograph by D.J. Dippie.

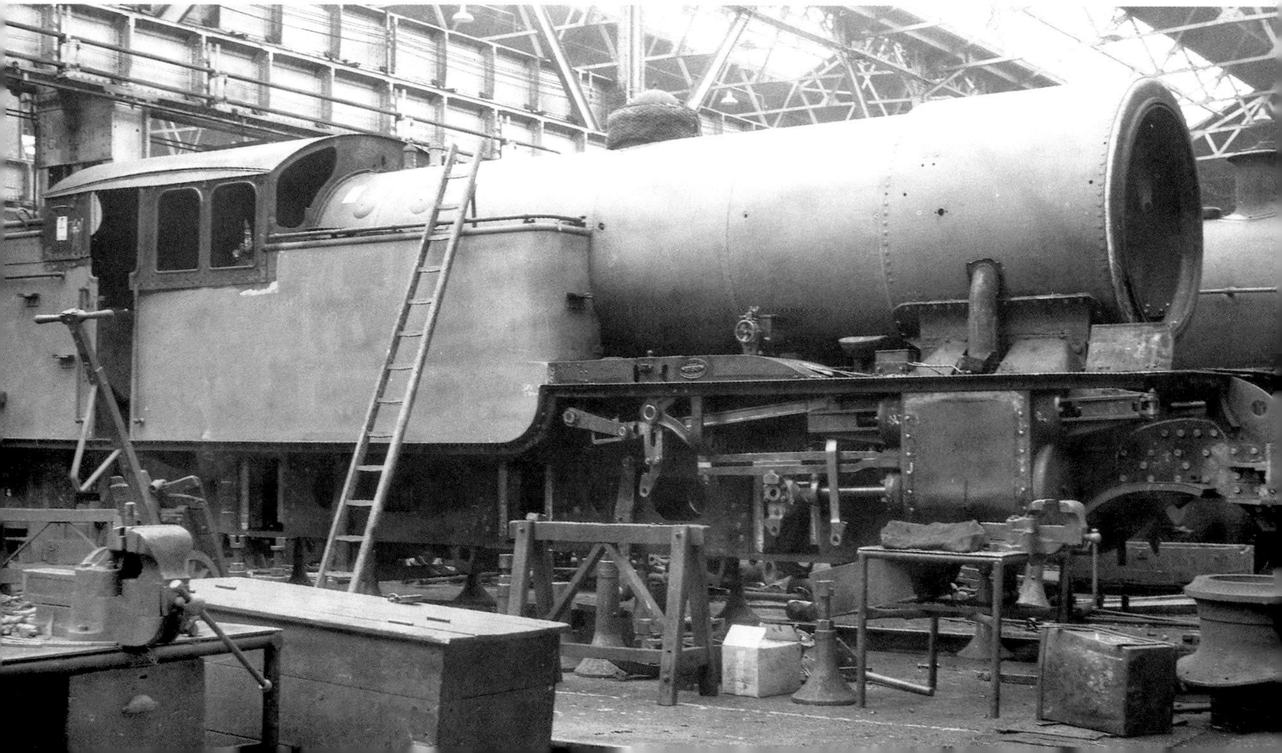

Above **DARLINGTON WORKS – NO. 68050**
View from Whessoe Road footbridge to Darlington Works on 9th July 1963. The line from the shops crossed over the road to reach the Shildon/Barnard Castle routes. J94 Class no. 68050 is at work shunting in the yard. Photograph by D.J. Dippie.

Below **DARLINGTON SHED – NO. 68046 AND NO. 68051**
Three J94 Class 0-6-0STs appear to be in store at Darlington shed. Two are identifiable: no. 68046 and no. 68051. The aforementioned was constructed at Vulcan Foundry in August 1945 and mainly worked at York under BR before arriving at Darlington in 1962 for the last two years in service. No. 68051 entered traffic a month later than no. 68046 from W.G. Bagnall and had several allocations in the 1950s/1960s. The final one to Darlington lasted just two months until condemned in June 1964 at the same time as no. 68046. Photograph by D.J. Dippie.

Above **DARLINGTON WORKS – NO. 60011**

Gresley A4 no. 60011 *Empire of India* was sent to Darlington for repair in April 1964 only for the works to condemn the locomotive. Awaiting dispatch to the scrapyard on 2nd May, no. 60011 is in the company of class mate no. 60020 *Guillemot* which was marked for the same fate. Photograph courtesy Rail-Online.

Below **DARLINGTON – NO. 65784**

A coal train passes through Darlington behind Worsdell J27 Class 0-6-0 no. 65784. The locomotive was constructed at Darlington Works in May 1906 and was withdrawn in August 1959. Under BR, Percy Main shed employed the engine. Photograph by Bill Reed.

Above DERWENTHAUGH COKE WORKS – NO. 59

On the west bank of the River Derwent near Winlaton Mill (south of Blaydon), the Consett Iron Company opened Derwenthaugh coke works in 1928. A locomotive shed was also established to house and service a small fleet of locomotives which worked at the site and sidings. No. 59 is pictured outside the structure in April 1970. Constructed by the Vulcan Foundry in 1945 for the War Department, the engine was later taken into stock by the National Coal Board. In the early 1970s, no. 59 fell out of use and was later scrapped. Derwenthaugh coke works closed in the 1980s and the site cleared. Photograph by Richard Pelham courtesy Rail Photoprints.

Opposite DURHAM STATION – NO. 69852

Raven's D Class 4-4-4T design (LNER H1) numbered 45 examples at Grouping and these engines were used on local passenger trains. Following the success of J.G. Robinson's 9N 4-6-2T (LNER A5) design in the North East after 1923, Gresley decided to reconstruct the H1 with another pair of coupled wheels – A8 Class – and all were converted between 1931 and 1936. No. 69852 started life at Darlington in November 1913 and became A8 in February 1936. The locomotive is seen at Durham station on 21st September 1958 reversing away with a train of empty stock. Sunderland-based at this time, in November 1959 the engine was condemned at the depot. Photograph by K. Wightman from the Dave Cobbe Collection courtesy Rail Photoprints.

Above **DERWENTHAUGH COKE WORKS – NO. 41**
Out of service at Derwenthaugh coke works engine shed in April 1970 is no. 41. The 0-6-0PT locomotive was constructed by Kitson & Co. in 1883, rebuilt by Hudswell Clarke at the turn of the century and preserved after withdrawal at the North Tyneside Steam Railway. Photograph by Richard Pelham courtesy Rail Photoprints.

Below **DURHAM STATION – NO. 67246**
Taking water from a platform column – with the tank overflowing – is Worsdell G5 Class 0-4-4T no. 67246. Seen at Durham station in June 1957, the engine was allocated to Sunderland and withdrawn there in November 1958. Photograph courtesy Colour-Rail.

Above DURHAM STATION – NO. 61901

Introduced by Gresley for mixed traffic duties on the Great Northern Railway, the H4 Class 2-6-0 became a Group Standard design after Grouping. Classified K3 by the LNER, a total of 193 were built to the design. No. 61901 was amongst forty ordered from Armstrong Whitworth & Co. in the mid-1930s. The locomotive is at Durham station with a train of empty stock on 15th October 1958. Photograph by D.J. Dippie.

Below DURHAM STATION – NO. 61454

An express freight is on the through line at Durham station on 16th July 1960, with Raven B16 Class no. 61454 of York. Photograph by D.J. Dippie.

Above DURHAM STATION – NO. 60138

Constructed at Darlington in December 1948, Peppercorn A1 no. 60138 *Boswell* went to York and remained in service there to October 1965. The engine is with an express at Durham station on 16th July 1960. Photograph by D.J. Dippie.

Below DURHAM – NO. 63874

Crossing the viaduct just south of Durham station is Thompson O1 2-8-0 no. 63874. Seen with a brake van on 24th September 1962, the locomotive had just two months left in traffic. Photograph by Tony Cooke courtesy Colour-Rail.

Above DURHAM STATION – NO. 60021
Durham (Gilesgate) was the first station in the city and was the end of a branch off the Leamside line from Pelaw to Ferryhill which opened in the mid-1840s. This station was replaced by the present facility in 1857 when the NER joined Durham with Bishop Auckland. The company later connected Durham to the East Coast Main Line when in 1872 a diversion was made from Ferryhill to run via Durham and Chester-le-Street to Newcastle. Gresley A4 no. 60021 *Wild Swan* is at Durham on 16th July 1961. Photograph by D.J. Dippie.

Below EASINGTON – NO. 90348
Between Sunderland and Hartlepool at Easington on 21st August 1967, WD 'Austerity' 2-8-0 no. 90348 has a coal train. Easington Colliery stands in the background on the left. Photograph courtesy Rail-Online.

EASINGTON – NO. 65894

Just north east of Easington – passing Shippersea Bay – Worsdell J27 no. 65894 has a loaded coal train in 1967. Photograph courtesy Rail-Online.

Above EASINGTON COLLIERY – NO. 65833

The settlement of Easington Colliery was established at the turn of the century with the construction of the pit. Worsdell J27 no. 65833 has coal from the colliery travelling over Hawthorn Dene viaduct in the 1960s. Photograph courtesy Rail-Online.

Below EASINGTON STATION – NO. 65856

Another Worsdell J27, no. 65856, is at Easington with a coal train. The locomotive is passing through the station on 8th May 1954 when allocated to Sunderland. Photograph by G.H. Hunt courtesy Colour-Rail.

Above FENCEHOUSES STATION – NO. 67265

Located between Penshaw and Leamside, Fencehouses station was operational from 1841 until 1964 when closed under the 'Beeching Axe'. Worsdell G5 Class 0-4-4T no. 67265 has a Sunderland to Durham local train at Fencehouses in the 1950s. Photograph courtesy Rail-Online.

Below GATESHEAD SHED – NO. 60868

On home ground and between duties at Gateshead shed on 24th October 1964 is Gresley V2 no. 60868. In the North East from July 1939, the locomotive's final year passed at Edinburgh St Margaret's depot. Photograph by G.S. Cocks courtesy Colour-Rail.

Above GATESHEAD SHED – NO. 67643

Originally intended for London suburban traffic, Gresley's V1 2-6-2T design was soon found to be of use elsewhere on the system and many were sent to Scotland and the North East. No. 67643 was built at Doncaster in July 1935 as the final engine of an order for ten placed during November 1933. Delivered to Parkhead shed, Glasgow, no. 67643 joined the North Eastern Region in the 1960s and was at Gateshead from December 1962 to November 1964. The locomotive is in the yard during the last year in traffic. Photograph by John Arnott-Brown courtesy A1 Steam Trust.

Below GATESHEAD SHED – NO. 67690

Another Gresley 2-6-2T, V3 no. 67690, is at Gateshead during 1964. In mid-1963, the V1s/V3s were concentrated at Gateshead for local stock and freight movements. Photograph by John Arnott-Brown courtesy A1 Steam Trust.

GATESHEAD EAST STATION – NO. 63346

A loaded coal train travels through Gateshead East station with Raven Q6 Class no. 63346 on 29th April 1966.
Photograph by A. Ferguson courtesy Colour-Rail.

Above GATESHEAD WORKS – NO. 63405

Raven Q6 Class no. 63405 is undergoing refurbishment work at Gateshead. Originally the NER's main workshops, Gateshead ceased construction in 1910 when the site became too cramped and Darlington took responsibility for the company's needs. Gateshead closed in 1932 following the trade depression, but reopened during the Second World War and the shops assisted with repairs through to 1959. Photograph courtesy Rail-Online.

Below GATESHEAD – NO. 60015

An express is at Gateshead with Gresley A4 no. 60015 *Quicksilver* on 1st August 1960. The train is southbound having come off the King Edward VII bridge. Photograph by D.J. Dippie.

GATESHEAD – NO. 6
Placed under the bridge carrying Regent Court
no. 60070 passes Gateshead in June 1961
Photograph courtesy Colour-Rail

Above GATESHEAD SHED – NO. 67628

Gresley V3 Class no. 67628 stands on a radiating line off the turntable in one of the abandoned roundhouses at Gateshead on 24th October 1964. Two buildings – dating from 1867 and 1877 – were demolished by BR in the mid-1950s, leaving two others with coverings for interior storage of engines. Photograph by Neville Simms from the Ranwell Collection courtesy Rail Photoprints.

Below GATESHEAD SHED – NO. 68723

A number of locomotives around the country were kept in special condition for shunting duties in major stations. At Newcastle, Worsdell J72 no. 68723 had NER livery for a number of years. Seen at Gateshead shed on 30th September 1963, the engine had been withdrawn for a week. Photograph courtesy Rail-Online.

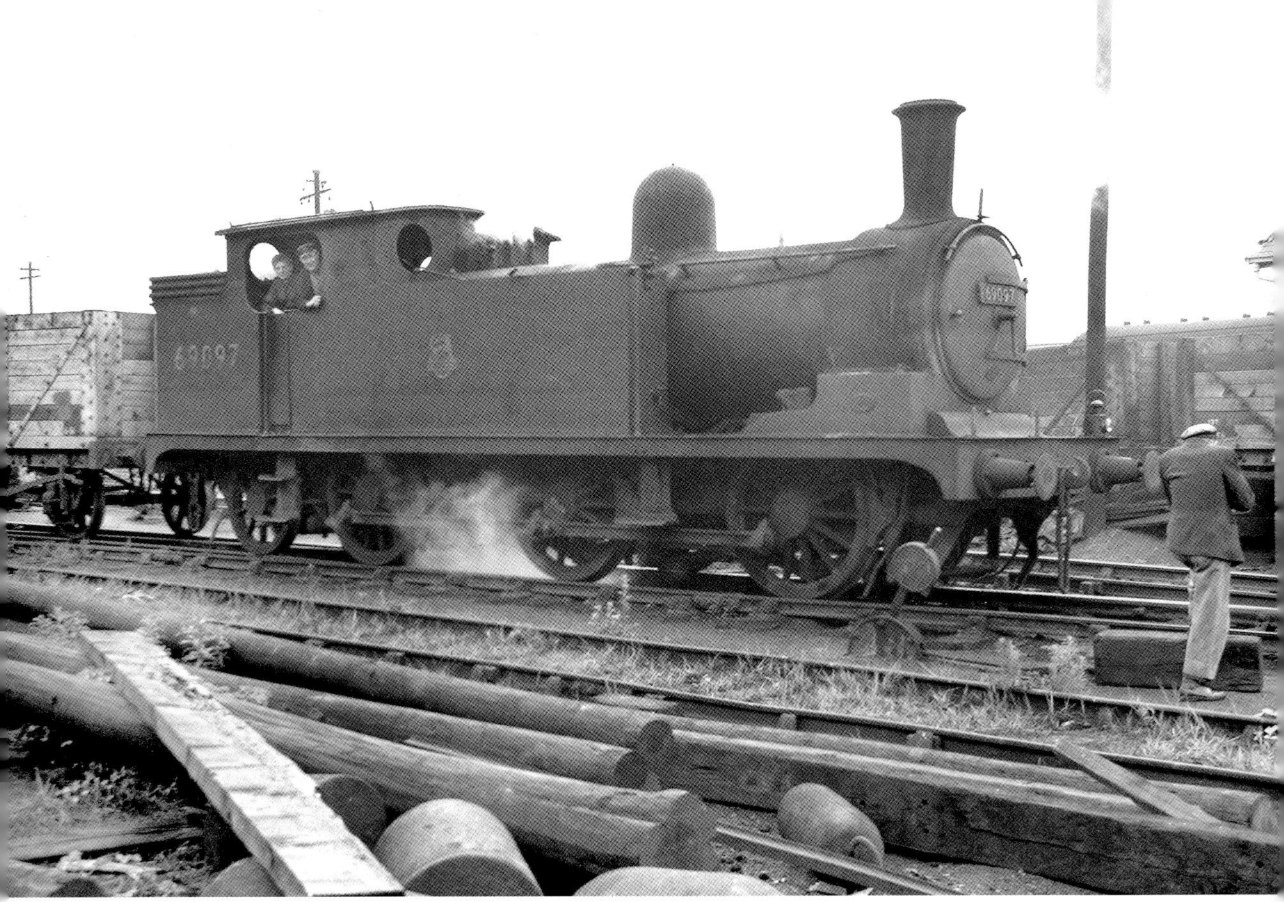
69097
69097

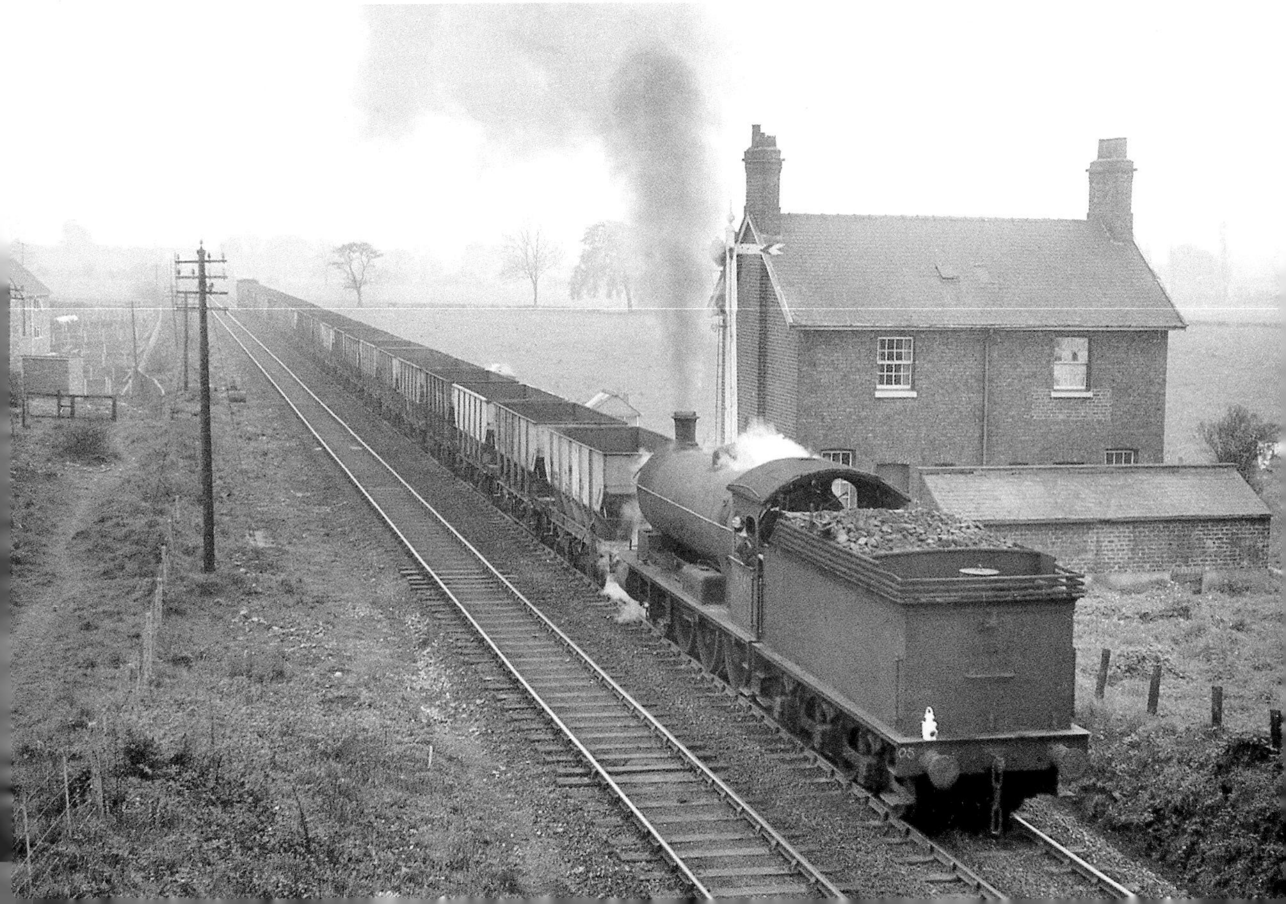

Above HARTBURN JUNCTION – NO. 60878

Just south of Stockton-on-Tees station, Hartburn Junction provided access to Thornaby via Hartburn East Curve. Gresley V2 no. 60878 is passing this on the right with a parcels train. Pictured on 25th January 1962, the locomotive was engaged at York and in service there to October when sent for scrap at Darlington Works. Photograph by David P. Williams courtesy Rail-Online.

Opposite above GATESHEAD SHED – NO. 69097

Introduced in the early 20th century, Worsdell's U Class 0-6-2T (LNER N10) featured similar specifications to contemporary goods engines, such as the P1 (LNER J25) 0-6-0. A total of 20 appeared from Darlington Works and no. 69097 was constructed as NER no. 1109 in December 1902. Though capable of passenger work, the class was kept to freight duties, such as local journeys and shunting in the many yards across the North East. In the unification of brakes during the 1930s, the N10s were given vacuum and steam brakes, but in the 1940s this became steam only rendering passenger duties extremely unlikely. At Grouping, no. 69097 was at Blaydon, then before the war worked at Bowes Bridge and by Nationalisation reached Gateshead. The locomotive remained there until condemned during April 1962. Seen on 11th June 1960, the engine is shunting at Gateshead shed. Photograph by D.J. Dippie.

Opposite below HARDWICK – NO. 63409

The Castle Eden Railway was built by the North Eastern Railway in the mid-1870s, leaving the Darlington to Stockton/Thornaby line and running northward to join the Hartlepool & Dock Railway between there and Ferryhill. The route was fully operational by 1880. Passenger services were later withdrawn in the 1930s and freight traffic discontinued in the early 1950s, though the line continued to carry some trains, including this one consisting of empty hopper wagons with Raven Q6 Class no. 63409 on 1st May 1961 at Hardwick, to the west of Stockton-on-Tees. The line was fully lifted in the late 1960s. Photograph courtesy Rail-Online.

Above HARTON – NO. 90445

The Stephenson Locomotive Society's Tees-side branch opted for the comfort of several brake vans and a WD 'Austerity' on a jaunt around East Durham's industrial lines on 15th May 1965. No. 90445 was used throughout the day and has the train at Harton near Tyne Dock. Photograph by Chris Davies courtesy Rail Photoprints.

Below HEATON SHED – NO. 60145

Nameless Peppercorn Pacific no. 60145 – originally *Saint Mungo* – is at Heaton shed in 1966. One of two class members in service at the start of the year, withdrawal of the engine occurred in March, though within a month no. 60145 was back at work from York. This lasted until mid-June and – despite a preservation proposal – *Saint Mungo* went to Hull for scrapping. Photograph by John Arnott-Brown courtesy A1 Steam Trust.

Above HEATON STATION – NO. 68747

Heaton (east of Newcastle station) was first served by a station on the main line to Edinburgh and the North Shields route from 1856. When track improvements occurred in the mid-1880s, a second station opened in 1887. Worsdell J72 Class no. 68747 is at Heaton station in the mid-1950s when employed at the local depot. Photograph courtesy Rail-Online.

Below HEATON SHED – NO. 60521

Thompson A2/3 Class Pacific no. 60521 *Watling Street* is at Heaton shed for servicing on 24th May 1961. The engine arrived at the depot from Gateshead in May 1960 and remained to October 1961. A year was spent at Tweedmouth before withdrawal. Photograph by D.J. Dippie.

Above HEATON SHED – NO. 60051

Approaching 40 years of age, Gresley A3 Pacific no. 60051 *Blink Bonny* is outside Heaton shed on 1st July 1964. The engine was built at Doncaster in November 1924 and was condemned in the same month of 1964 at Gateshead. No. 60051 had seen many changes during this period: long-travel valves; tender; livery; sheds; A1 to A3 conversion in November 1945; Kylchap double chimney; smoke deflectors; etc. Early in 1965, no. 60051 was cut up at North Blyth. Photograph by Philip Jackson courtesy A1 Steam Trust.

Opposite above HENDON JUNCTION – NO. 63437

Hendon Junction was located amidst the lines serving Sunderland Docks and connected the line from Penshaw and the north, as well as the routes from Hartlepool and Stockton-on-Tees. Raven Q6 Class no. 63437 is at the junction ready to collect a train on 15th May 1965. Photograph by Chris Davies courtesy Rail Photoprints.

Opposite below HENDON JUNCTION – NO. 62030

Another locomotive caught at Hendon Junction on 15th May 1965 was Peppercorn K1 no. 62030, which has charge of a brake van. Completed at the North British Locomotive Company in August 1949, no. 62030 reported for duty at Blaydon shed and was there subsequently for 13 years. When pictured, the locomotive was Sunderland-allocated and condemned there in August 1965. Photograph by Chris Davies courtesy Rail Photoprints.

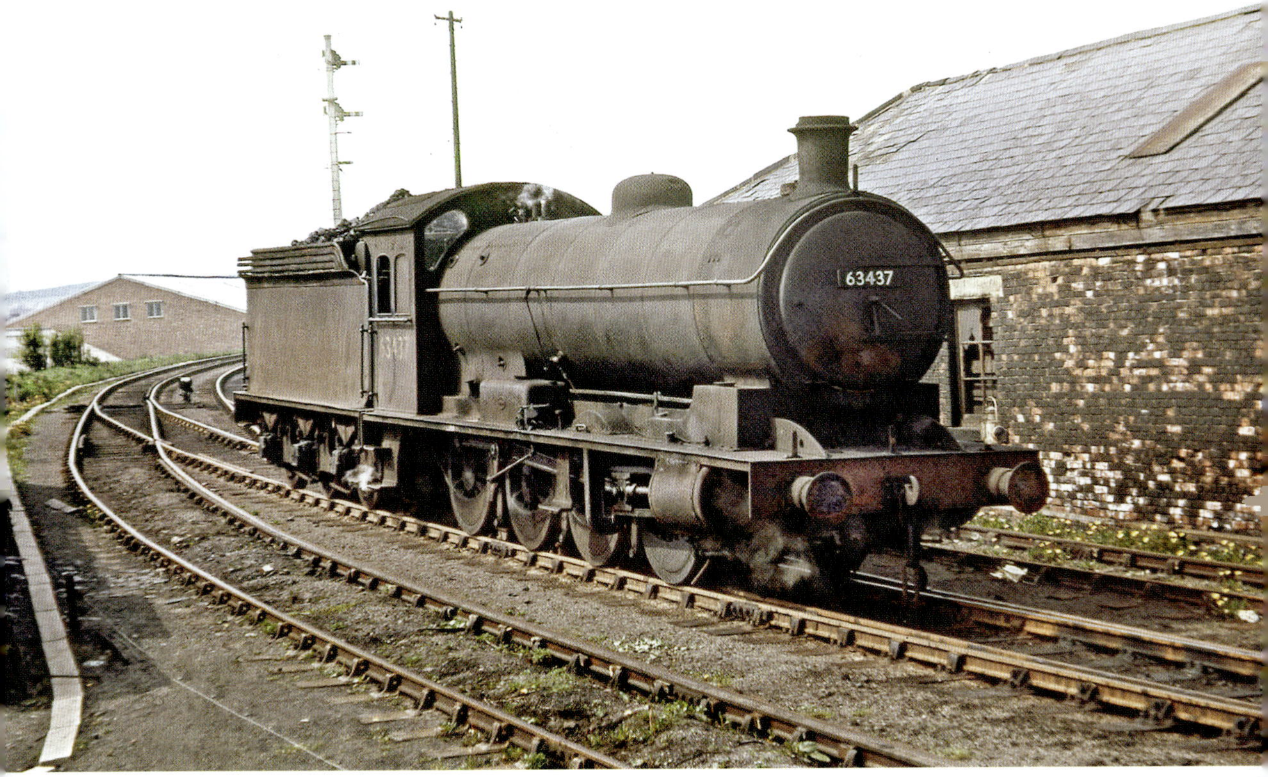
63437

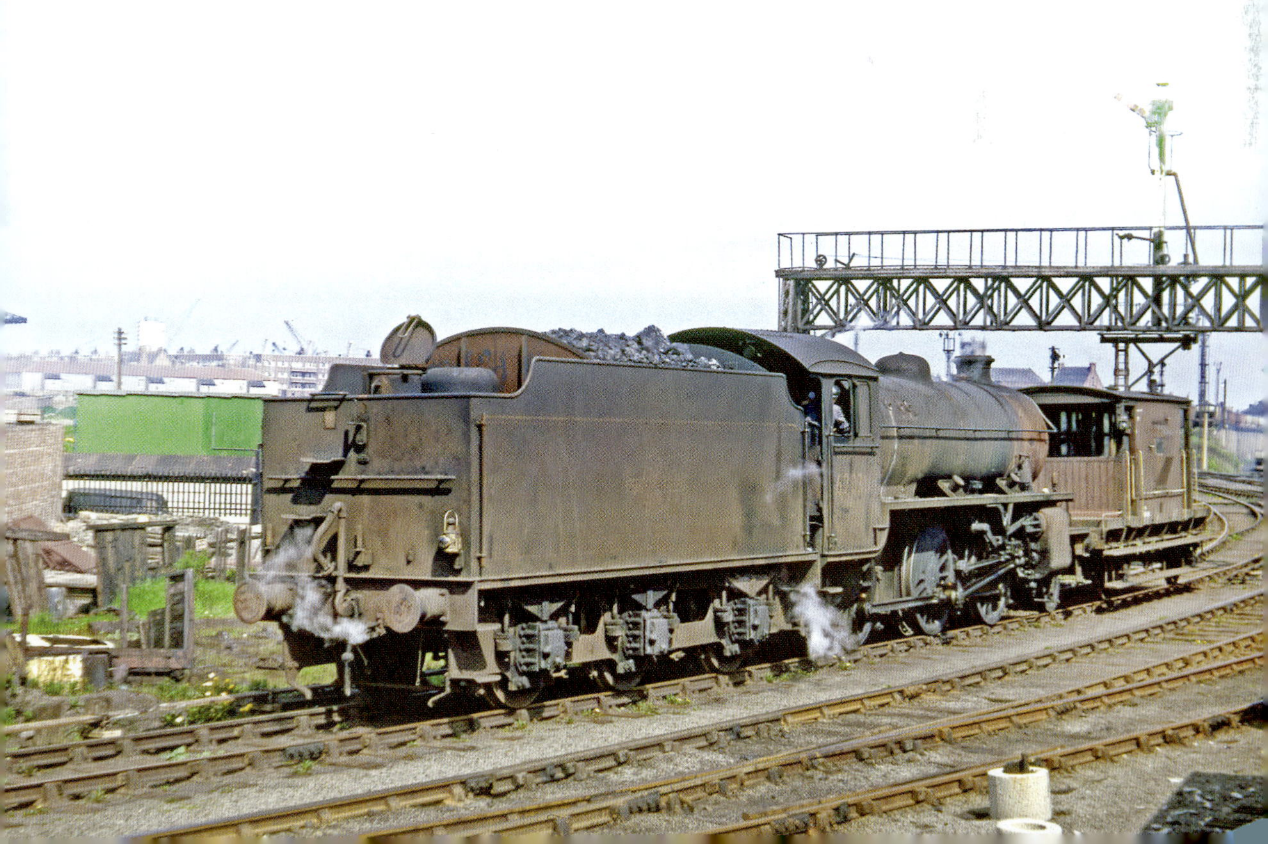

LONDONDERRY JUNCTION – NO. 65853
Crew and guard take a break adjacent to Londonderry Junction signal box, Sunderland on 15th May 1965. Worsdell J27 no. 65853 is the locomotive. Photograph by Chris Davies courtesy Rail Photoprints.

Above HEPSCOTT STATION – NO. 65811

The Blyth & Tyne Railway served much of the area north of Newcastle, including the small village of Hepscott with a few hundred residents. Located to the east of Morpeth, a station was built at Hepscott in April 1858 and open to passengers until 1950, with freight calling until 1964. A train of coal hoppers is at Hepscott in 1966 and drawn by Worsdell J27 no. 65811. Photograph courtesy Rail-Online.

Below HEXHAM SHED – NO. 67268

Worsdell G5 Class 0-4-4T no. 67268 is prepared for the next duty at Hexham shed in 1953. The locomotive was in service for a further two years. Photograph courtesy Rail-Online.

Above LINTON COLLIERY – NO. 37
North of Ashington, Linton Colliery was established in 1894 and went on to employ around 1,500. Robert Stephenson & Hawthorns 0-6-0ST no. 37 has a train of coal hoppers from the colliery at Portland Junction on 1st June 1966. Photograph by Hugh Ballantyne courtesy Rail Photoprints.

Opposite LAMBTON COLLIERY – NO. 31
Kitson & Co. 0-6-2T, Lambton no. 31, is shunting coal hoppers at Lambton Colliery on 20th September 1965. Photograph by Hugh Ballantyne courtesy Rail Photoprints.

Above MARCHEYS HOUSE – NO. 65819

South of Ashington at Marcheys House, Worsdell J27 Class no. 65819 has a coal train for Cambois Power Station (also known as Blyth Power Station) on 1st June 1966. The locomotive was in traffic for almost 60 years, being erected by the North British Locomotive Company in May 1908 and withdrawn from Blyth shed in September 1966. The engine looks particularly tired at this point with considerable scorching to the smokebox, even though an effort has been made to 'spruce up' the buffer beam. Photograph by Hugh Ballantyne courtesy Rail Photoprints.

Opposite LAMBTON RAILWAY – NO. 58

The Earls of Durham – the Lambton family – drew on the riches present in their land by sinking several pits to reach the coal measures in the area. This began in the 17th/18th centuries and soon saw a wagonway built to transport the product to the wider area, as well as the River Wear for movement further afield. A small section between Fatfield and Cox Green opened in the late 1730s. Steam first ran on the Lambton Railway in 1814 and the concern subsequently grew to 70 miles of route with access to Sunderland Docks. At the height of the Lambton Colliery Co. several dozen locomotives were at work and dedicated repair shops were established at Philadelphia. No. 58 is seen on the Lambton Railway in the mid-1960s. Photograph courtesy Rail-Online.

Above MARSDEN QUARRY

The area around the village of Marsden (on the Durham Coast) was originally exploited for limestone deposits. Later, Whitburn Colliery was sunk and all the concerns were eventually taken over by the Harton Colliery Co. An industrial railway served both the quarry and colliery and an unidentified 0-6-0ST is with quarry wagons on 17th September 1962. Photograph by John Briggs courtesy A1 Steam Trust.

Below MELDON STATION – NO. 65893

West of Morpeth at Meldon station, Worsdell J27 Class 0-6-0 no. 65893 is performing shunting duties in 1964. Meldon closed to freight two years later – passenger services were withdrawn 12 years earlier. Photograph by John Arnott-Brown courtesy A1 Steam Trust.

Above MIDDLESBROUGH DOCKS – NO. 69006
A train of bolster wagons, which looks to be carrying steel beams, is at Middlesbrough Docks with Worsdell J72 Class 0-6-0T no. 69006 on 9th January 1962. The engine was based locally at Thornaby though was soon to move on to Darlington following the introduction of diesel shunters. Photograph by David P. Williams courtesy Rail-Online.

Below MIDDLESBROUGH DOCKS – NO. 5732
Still with LNER number on 9th July 1949, Worsdell J26 Class 0-6-0 no. 5732 took the BR number in November 1950. The engine has a freight train at Middlesbrough Docks. Photograph by T.B. Owen courtesy Colour-Rail.

Above MIDDLESBROUGH SHED – NO. 63375

Stabling facilities were erected by the Stockton & Darlington Railway near Middlesbrough station. These were later superseded by a trio of roundhouses built a short distance away to the east, c. 1870. Damage sustained during the war remained unrepaired until closure in 1958. Three locomotives are 'on shed' here in early July 1956: Raven A8 Class 4-6-2T no. 69892; Raven Q6 Class no. 63375; Worsdell J25 Class 0-6-0 no. 65720. The last two were Middlesbrough-allocated and moved to Thornaby when the depot closed, whilst no. 69892 was visiting from Saltburn-by-the-Sea. Photograph from the Gordon Edgar Collection courtesy Rail Photoprints.

Opposite above MIDDLESBOUGH STATION – NO. 65743

In the early 1900s, Worsdell developed his NER P1 Class 0-6-0 to carry a significantly larger boiler. The P1 boiler measured 4 ft 3 in. diameter whilst the new locomotives, NER P2 (LNER J26), had a boiler 5 ft 6 in. diameter. Darlington constructed 30 in 1904/1905, whilst Gateshead added a further 20 in 1905. The P2s were mainly settled in their roles of moving freight and mineral traffic around the North East, with the only significant change made to the P2s during their time in service concerning the boiler. With slightly different tube arrangement and firebox design, the P3-type boiler was fitted to several class members in the 1910s and 1920s, including no. 65743 as NER no. 1130 in June 1915. Under the LNER, the P3 boiler was again redesigned and no. 65743 was the first J26 equipped with the diagram 57A boiler during October 1939. Though a superheated version of this was made, no J26 was never superheated. No. 65743 has a westbound freight at Middlesbrough station on 15th March 1962. The locomotive was amongst the last class withdrawals in June when the J26 became extinct. Photograph courtesy Colour-Rail.

Opposite below MIDDLESBROUGH STATION – NO. 64758

With brake van near Sussex Street level crossing over the lines at Middlesbrough station, Gresley J39 Class 0-6-0 no. 64758 is seen on 15th March 1962. The locomotive was erected at Darlington in September 1928 and the first allocation was to Doncaster depot. At this time, the engine, as LNER no. 2705, was provided with a Group Standard 3,500-gallon tender with 5½-ton coal capacity. This type was connected to the locomotive until October 1953 when switched with an NER 4,125-gallon tender, with space for 5½ tons of coal, which had been reused from Raven's Pacifics when the class was scrapped in the 1930s. Tender no. 8901 was paired and this had been with J39 Class no. 1475 when new and briefly with another class mate in 1953 and a J38 in the same year before coupled to 64758. Both were condemned at Thornaby in November 1962. Photograph courtesy Colour-Rail.

Above MORPETH – NO. 65893

Morpeth saw the convergence of three lines. The main route from Newcastle to Edinburgh passed through, whilst the Wansbeck Railway branch from Scotsgap joined from the west and the Blyth & Tyne arrived to the east. The station opened in 1847 and is still in use though the westward connection is lost. No. 65893 is at Morpeth in 1964. Photograph by John Arnott-Brown courtesy A1 Steam Trust.

Below NEWCASTLE STATION – NO. 63363

Light engine on the avoiding lines around Newcastle station is Raven Q6 Class no. 63363. Seen on 17th June 1965, the locomotive was Tyne Dock-allocated and withdrawn there in September 1966. Photograph by Bill Reed.

Above NEWCASTLE STATION – NO. 43057
The RCTS-organised 'Blyth & Tyne' railtour is ready to depart from Newcastle station on 19th September 1965 behind Ivatt Class 4MT no. 43057. Photograph by Geoff Warnes.

Below NEWCASTLE STATION – NO. 67646
An overcast Saturday, 18th July 1964, has Gresley V3 no. 67646 between duties at Newcastle station. The locomotive lasted to the end of the year on the roster at Gateshead shed. Photograph by David Christie.

Above NEWCASTLE STATION – NO. 60504

Thompson A2/2 Class Pacific no. 60504 *Mons Meg* is with a passenger train at Newcastle station on 24th May 1958. Starting life as a Gresley P2 Class 2-8-2, which were used between Edinburgh and Aberdeen, the locomotive was rebuilt as a Pacific by Edward Thompson in November 1944 to provide a basis for his proposed mixed traffic Pacific. In this form, the design proved prone to slip with heavy loads on the adverse gradients on that route and no. 60504 was displaced to Peterborough New England shed for tasks within the engine's capabilities. *Mons Meg* was scrapped at Doncaster following withdrawal in January 1961. Photograph by D.J. Dippie.

Opposite above NEWCASTLE STATION – NO. 65882

A long train of coal hopper wagons trails behind Worsdell J27 Class 0-6-0 no. 65882 at Newcastle station on 19th August 1965. Amongst the later group of Worsdell's P3 Class, the locomotive was equipped with a superheater when erected at Darlington Works in August 1922. Whilst many classes were retrospectively fitted with the apparatus to improve performance, many of the P3s were gradually provided with a saturated boiler and just six of the thirty-five superheated locomotives retained the original arrangement through their careers. No. 65882 ran until February 1944 when given the saturated diagram 57A boiler. The superheated engines also had piston valves from new in place of slide valves which did not perform as well with high temperature steam. These appear to have been retained when conversions took place. No. 65822 was allocated to North Blyth when pictured, yet had two months at Sunderland before condemned in September 1967. Photograph by Bill Reed.

Opposite below NEWCASTLE STATION – NO. 60877

A parcels train has paused for water on the avoiding lines at Newcastle station on 4th June 1960. Gresley V2 no. 60877's tender is in need and this was of the Group Standard variety with 4,200-gallon water capacity and coal space for 7 tons 10 cwt. The locomotive has also suffered from a defective cylinder block. When the V2 was designed, Gresley adopted North Eastern Railway practice of casting the three cylinders as a whole unit, though when faults developed the casting had to be completely replaced. A number of V2s were affected and no. 60877 received separate castings for the three cylinders in January 1959. This was outwardly distinguished by the steam pipes, which were originally internal for the monobloc. No. 60877 was allocated to York a year earlier and lasted there until February 1966. Photograph by D.J. Dippie.

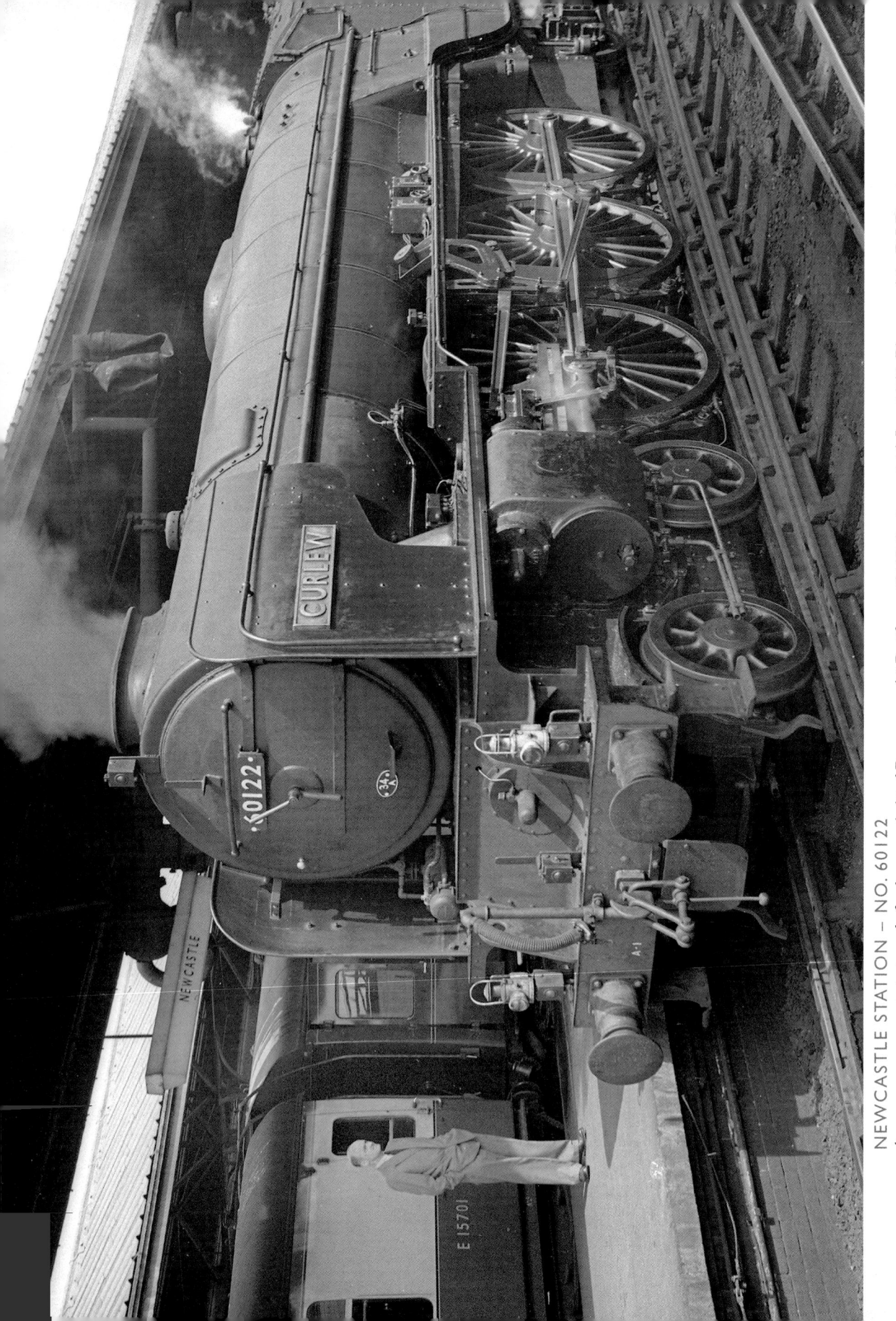

NEWCASTLE STATION – NO. 60122

An express passenger train is ready for departure behind Peppercorn A1 Pacific no. 60122 *Curlew* on 14th June 1958. Photograph by D.J. Dippie.

Above NEWCASTLE STATION – NO. 60918
Gresley V2 no. 60918 is coupled to a passenger service at Newcastle on 14th June 1958. The engine was one of the few class members with a sole allocation, which in this instance was York. Photograph by D.J. Dippie.

Below NEWCASTLE STATION – NO. 60028
Whilst a Monday-Friday service, the 'Elizabethan' set ran on Saturday as a nameless train stopping at Newcastle; technically the headboard should be removed or reversed. Gresley A4 no. 60028 *Walter K. Whigham* has the train on 5th September 1959. Photograph by D.J. Dippie.

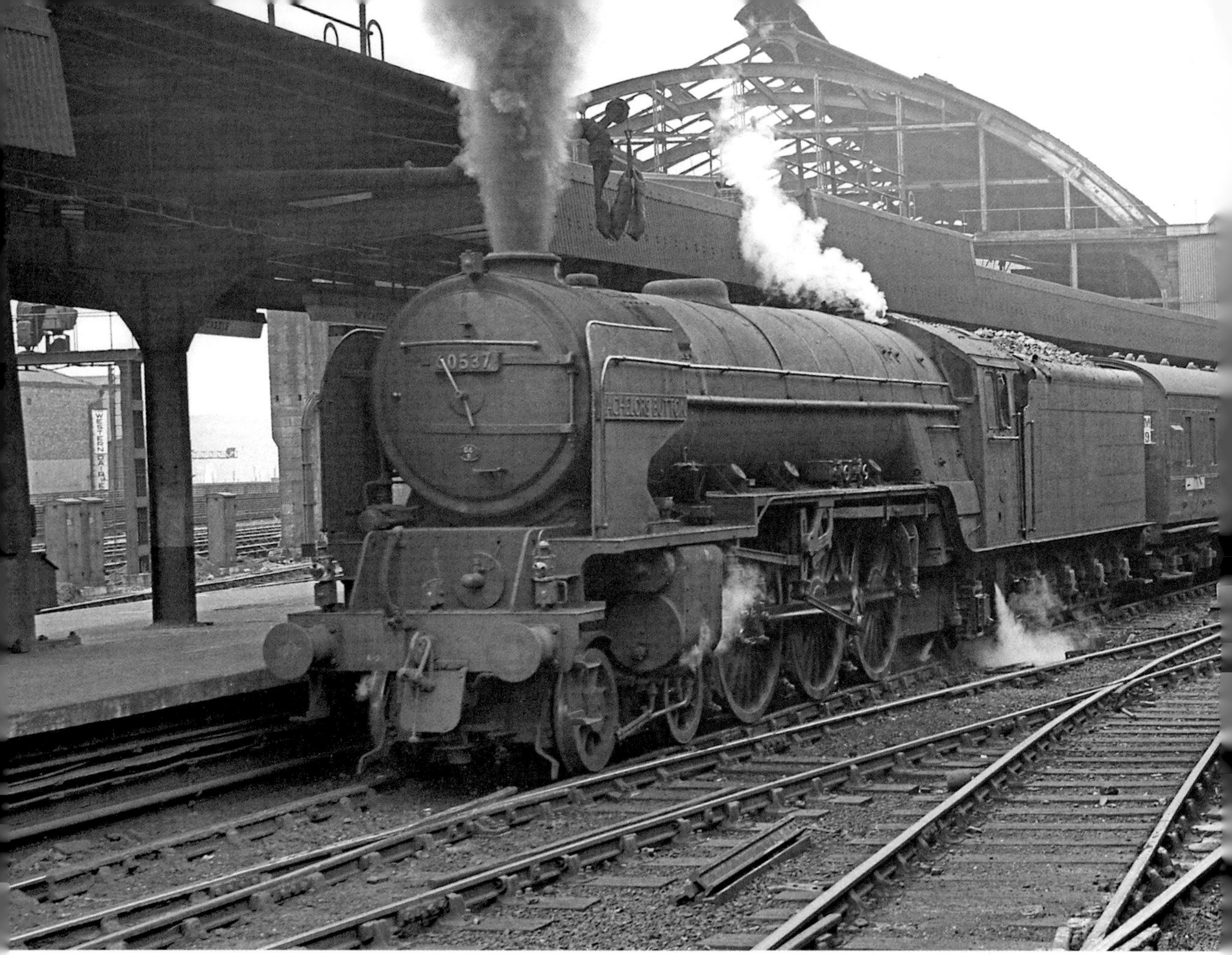
60537

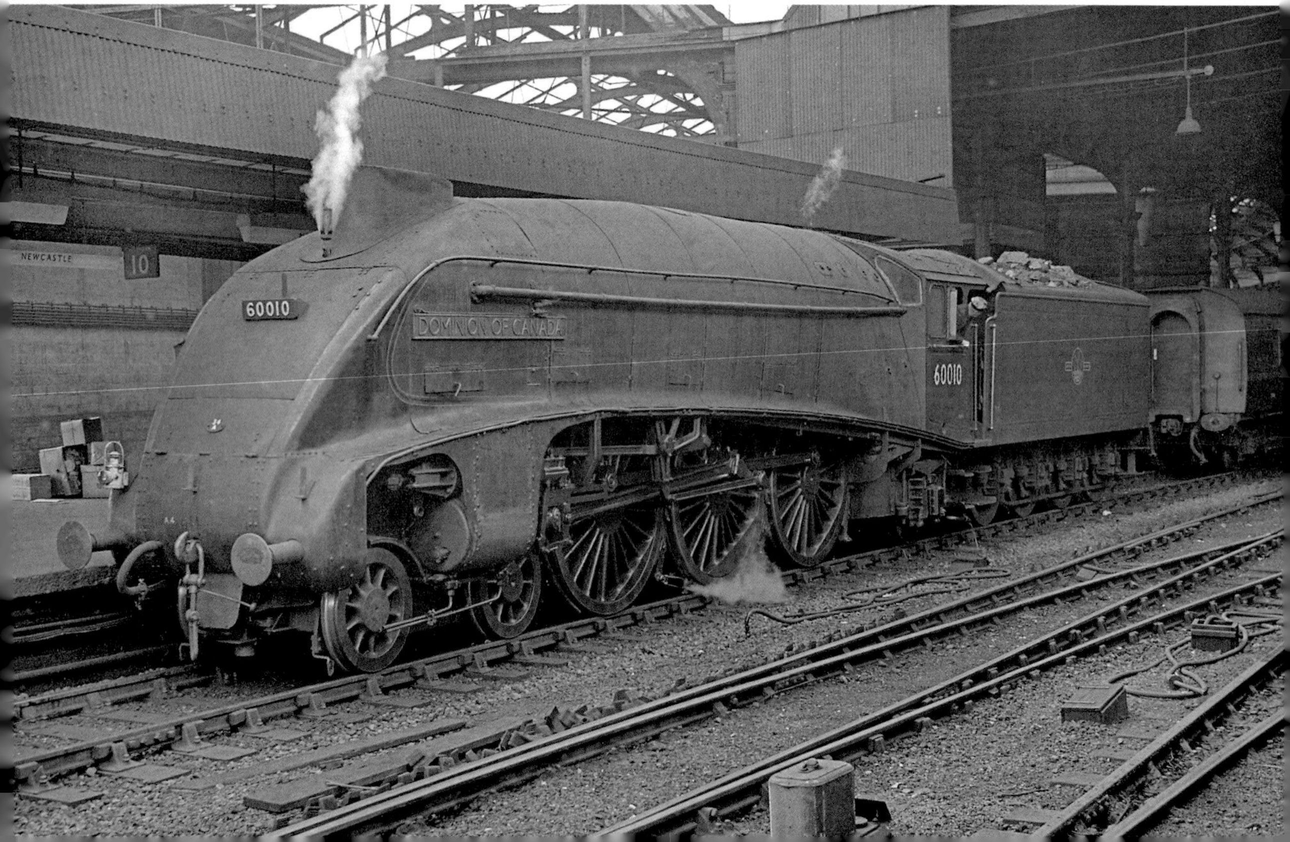
NEWCASTLE
10
60010
DOMINION OF CANADA
60010

Opposite above NEWCASTLE STATION – NO. 60537
Edward Thompson's A2/3s proved troublesome in service, so when A.H. Peppercorn succeeded him as Chief Mechanical Engineer of the LNER in 1946, the 15 class members on order were redesigned. No. 60537 *Bachelors Button* was amongst the last built at Doncaster in June 1948 and delivered new to Leeds Copley Hill. Peppercorn A2s later replaced Thompson A2/2s in Scotland and no. 60537 was selected to transfer, moving to Aberdeen in 1949, then Edinburgh Haymarket in 1951. The locomotive has an express here at Newcastle station on 11th June 1960. Photograph by D.J. Dippie.

Opposite below NEWCASTLE STATION – NO. 60010
Gresley A4 Class Pacific no. 60010 *Dominion of Canada* is uncoupled from an express at Newcastle station on 11th June 1960. The locomotive looks ready to take on the train judging from the amount of coal in the tender. Photograph by D.J. Dippie.

Below NEWCASTLE QUAYSIDE – NO. 68713
Worsdell J72 Class 0-6-0T no. 68713 and footplateman take a break on the Newcastle Quayside branch on 10th June 1961. The locomotive was Heaton-allocated at this time and withdrawal occurred there in October 1961. Photograph by D.J. Dippie.

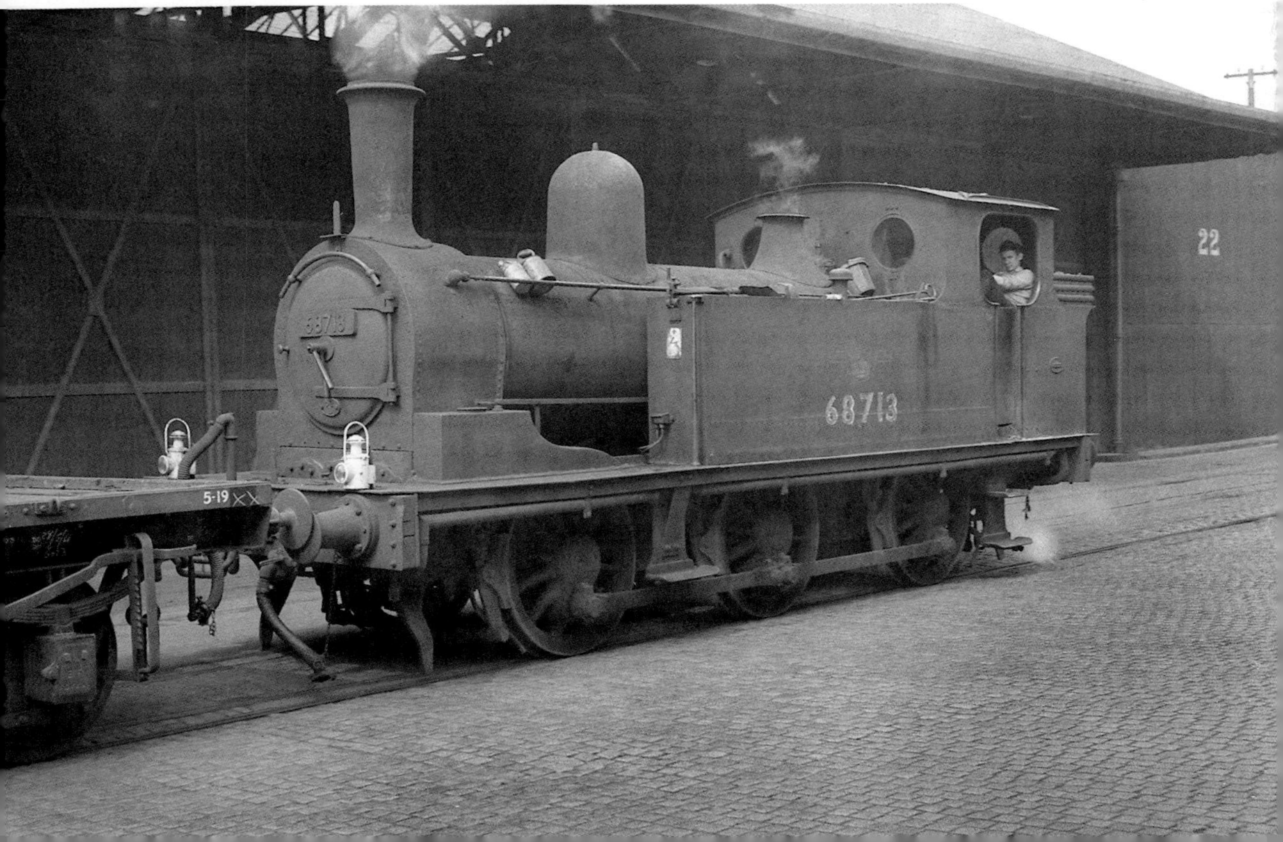

Above NEWCASTLE STATION – NO. 67652 AND NO. 67647

A scene at Newcastle station, captured during the mid-1950s, which has two Gresley V1 Class 2-6-2T joined at the head of an unidentified passenger train. The pilot engine is no. 67652 which has been fitted with a V3 boiler and this fact is noted on the buffer beam. The locomotive had the boiler from February 1952 whilst no. 67647 (coupled to the train) was made a V3 in December 1959. Both were mainly Heaton locomotives during the 1950s. No. 67652 was withdrawn from Gateshead in December 1963, whilst no. 67647 went from Heaton at the start of that year. Photograph from the Dave Cobbe Collection courtesy Rail Photoprints.

Opposite NEWCASTLE STATION – NO. 60516

As the P2 to A2/2 rebuilds provided a basis for Thompson's 6 ft 2 in. mixed traffic Pacific, authorisation was given to move to production locomotives. The first of these was no. 60500 *Edward Thompson* which appeared before the engine's namesake retired in 1946. Fourteen more followed before production shifted to Peppercorn's A2 design at Nationalisation. No. 60516 *Hycilla* was built at Doncaster in November 1946 and new to Heaton shed. A total of nine from the fifteen were employed in the North East, with Gateshead and York sharing the class members. In the area, the class had regular express diagrams, including named train duties – such as the 'Queen of Scots' Pullman – and freight duties northward to Edinburgh, also southward, including to Hull, and Leeds. No. 60516 moved over to Gateshead in the early 1950s, though returned to Heaton when the class was displaced from the aforementioned as dieselisation increased. York took *Hycilla* soon after and used the engine to November 1962 when condemned for scrap. No. 60516 is at Newcastle station with an express passenger train on 6th June 1960. Photograph by D.J. Dippie.

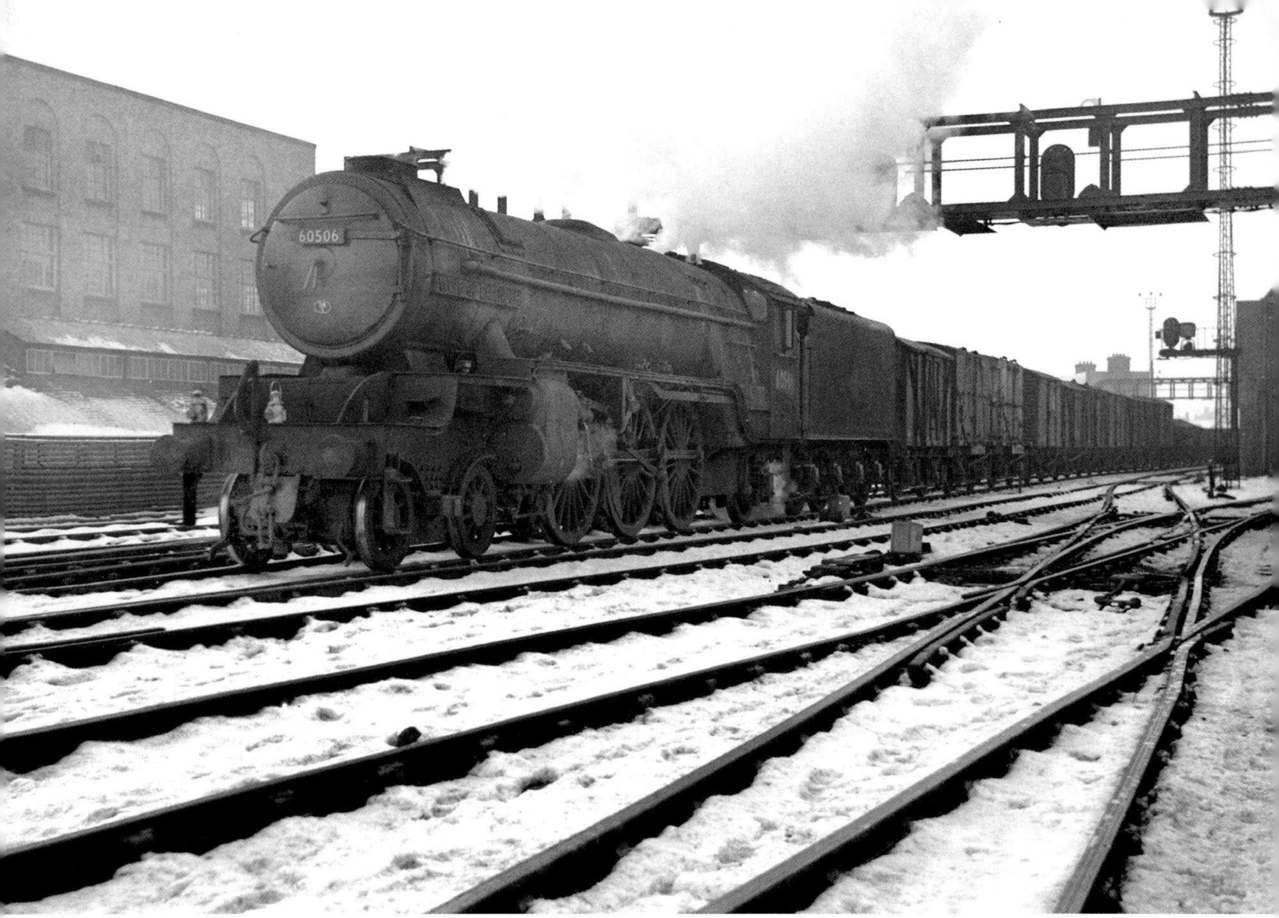
60506

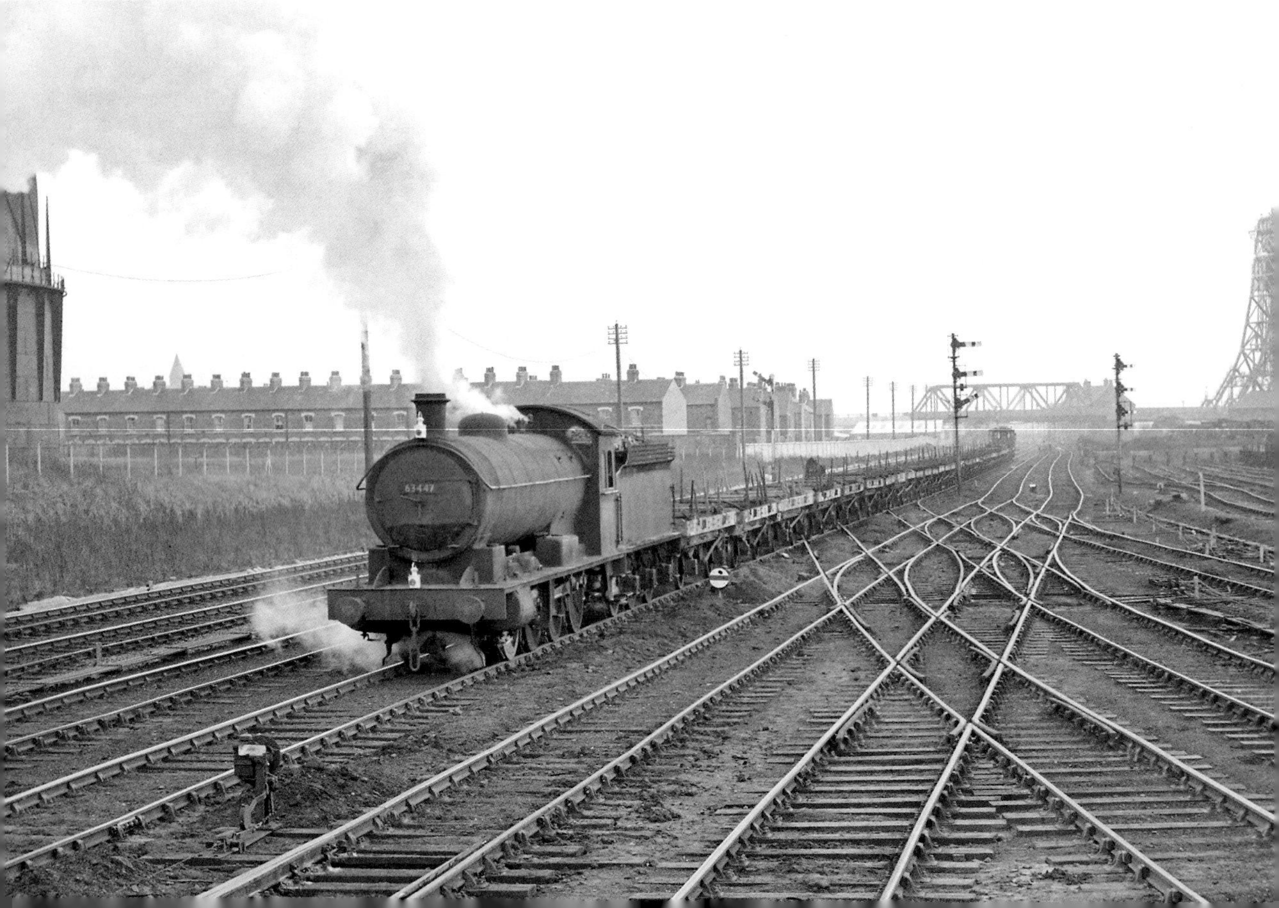
63447

Above NORTH BLYTH SHED – NO. 62027

Maintenance appears to be in progress on Peppercorn K1 2-6-0 no. 62027 on 14th July 1966 as the boiler washout plugs are removed. The locomotive had gone three years from the last general repair at Doncaster Works and would be in traffic for several months further before condemned at North Blyth shed in March 1967. Photograph courtesy Rail-Online.

Opposite above NEWCASTLE STATION – NO. 60506

An express freight trails behind Thompson A2/2 no. 60506 *Wolf of Badenoch* at Newcastle on a wintry day, 13th February 1960. The locomotive was approaching a year left in traffic as withdrawal occurred in April 1961. Built at Doncaster in September 1936 as part of Gresley's P2 Class 2-8-2s, LNER no. 2006 *Wolf of Badenoch* was rebuilt as a Pacific in April 1944. At this time the rebuilds were nameless, though the plates were soon after fitted, with no. 2006 rechristened in June of that year. After leaving Scotland in 1949, the engine was employed at Peterborough New England until sent for scrapping at Doncaster. Photograph by D.J. Dippie.

Opposite below NEWPORT – NO. 63447

Raven Q6 Class 0-8-0 no. 63447 is eastbound and heading towards Middlesbrough through Newport on 10th February 1962. In the background on the right is the Tees Newport lift bridge dating from 1934 and used for road traffic. Since the late 1980s, the bridge is set in the lowered position and no longer rises. No. 63447 was based locally at Thornaby depot and in April 1963 was withdrawn there. Photograph by David P. Williams courtesy Rail-Online.

NORTH BLYTH SHED

A view inside the roundhouse at North Blyth shed during October 1965 featuring: Peppercorn K1 no. 62024; Worsdell J27 no. 65801; Worsdell J27 no. 65809. Photograph courtesy Rail Photoprints.

Above NORTH BLYTH – NO. 43117
Departing from North Blyth sidings with a train of hopper wagons during June 1967 is Ivatt 4MT Class 2-6-0 no. 43117. Photograph from the Gordon Edgar Collection courtesy Rail Photoprints.

Below NORTON – NO. 63426
Just north of Stockton-on-Tees at Norton, Raven Q6 Class no. 63426 has a mineral train for Tees Yard on 20th January 1962. Photograph by David P. Williams courtesy Rail-Online.

HE IS A
L-OF-A-DRIVER

CO-OPERATIVE WHOLESALE SOCIETY LIMITED
DRYSALTERY WORKS
62023

Above PELAW STATION – NO. 63458

An eastbound train of coal hoppers passes through Pelaw station around 1967 behind Raven Q6 Class no. 63458. Built at Armstrong Whitworth & Co. in March 1921, the locomotive survived to July 1967. Under BR, no. 63458 worked from Gateshead Borough Gardens, Blaydon, Sunderland and Tyne Dock. Photograph courtesy Rail-Online.

Opposite above PALLION SHIPYARD

William Doxford & Sons was established at Pallion to the north west of Sunderland in 1840 and the site was an active shipbuilder to the late 1980s. One of the locomotives used at the site was Hawthorn Leslie 0-4-0CT *Pallion* seen here around 1970. Steam ceased to be used in the yard from 1971. Photograph courtesy Rail Photoprints.

Opposite below PELAW STATION – NO. 62023

Peppercorn K1 Class 2-6-0 no. 62023 is at Pelaw station with a mineral train on 21st June 1967. Located east of Gateshead, the first station at Pelaw was opened in 1839 on the Brandling Junction Railway which delivered coal to the Tyne. The station went on to be resited and rebuilt twice, with the last instance occurring in 1896 as part of line improvements. Pelaw was operational until the late 1970s but has since been resurrected as part of the Metro line. No. 62023 had a week left in service. Photograph by David Christie.

Left PELTON

West of Chester-le-Street at Pelton, NCB 0-6-0T no. 5 *Major* is light engine on 17th September 1962. The locomotive was new from Kitson & Co. in 1905 and delivered to Beamish Colliery. When pictured, no. 5 was employed nearby at Handen Hold Colliery and had been recently rebuilt five years earlier. No. 5 survived to the end of the decade and was then scrapped. Photograph by John Briggs courtesy A1 Steam Trust.

Opposite page PELAW – NO. 92099

Shunting at Pelaw in July 1966 is BR Standard Class 9F no. 92099. The locomotive had one allocation to Tyne Dock and this lasted from new in July 1956 to September 1966. Photograph courtesy Rail Photoprints.

Below PELTON

NCB no. 4 *Linhope* is at Pelton on 17th September 1962. The 0-6-0T locomotive was constructed by Robert Stephenson & Co. in 1895 as works no. 2822. Photograph by John Briggs courtesy A1 Steam Trust.

Opposite above **PENSHAW – NO. 31**

In the early 20th century, the Lambton Colliery Co. purchased several new 0-6-2T locomotives from Kitson & Co. No. 31 was received new in 1907 with works no. 4533. A feature particular to LCC locomotives was the rounded cab which was required to allow access to certain parts of the line owing to a narrow tunnel. No. 31 is at work near Penshaw with a short train of wooden coal wagons on 9th June 1966. Photograph by Peter Fitton courtesy Rail Photoprints.

Opposite below **PERCY MAIN – NO. 65813**

The crew of Worsdell J27 no. 65813 are in conference with the signalmen inside Engine Shed signal box at Percy Main on 24th August 1961. The box was nestled amidst lines connecting the different parts of Northumberland Docks, as well as the connection to Albert Edward Dock and Percy Main locomotive shed, where no. 65813 was allocated at the time. Photograph by D.J. Dippie.

Below **PERCY MAIN – NO. 65814**

A train of empty hopper wagons passes Percy Main behind Worsdell J27 Class no. 65814 on 23rd June 1962. The engine was local at this time and was later at North Blyth for a year before withdrawal in June 1966. Photograph by Ian Turnbull courtesy Rail Photoprints.

PERCY MAIN – NO. 65795

View northward from Engine Shed Junction, Percy Main, around the mid-1960s. The depot is in the background behind Howdon Road bridge, while Worsdell J27 no. 65795 is on the curve to Northumberland Dock. Photograph by D.J. Dippie.

Above PERCY MAIN SHED – NO. 65791
Standing inside the derelict shed at Percy Main in the mid-1960s is Worsdell J27 no. 65791. The engine was in service there to October 1964. Photograph by D.J. Dippie.

Below PERCY MAIN – NO. 65789 AND NO. 63429
Two locomotives at Percy Main on 1st July 1963 are Worsdell J27 no. 65789 and Raven Q6 no. 63429. Both worked from North Blyth shed at this time. Photograph by Philip Jackson courtesy A1 Steam Trust.

Above PHILADELPHIA
NCB no. 42 reverses to collect a train of coal on 7th July 1967. Photograph by Peter Fitton courtesy Rail Photoprints.

Opposite PHILADELPHIA
Loaded coal wagons trail behind Lambton Collieries 0-6-2T locomotive no. 42 at Philadelphia on 7th July 1967. The engine was erected by Robert Stephenson & Co. in 1920 and was in service until May 1970 when scrapped. Photograph by Peter Fitton courtesy Rail Photoprints.

PONTOP CROSSING – NO. 63712

Thompson O1 Class 2-8-0 no. 63712 is at Pontop Crossing with a coal train on 4th November 1960. The locomotive was allocated to Tyne Dock and has been fitted with Westinghouse equipment as a result. Photograph by D.J. Dippie.

Above PONTOP CROSSING – NO. 92062

A Consett to Tyne Dock iron ore train is at Pontop Crossing on 28th September 1962 with BR Standard Class 9F no. 92062. Photograph by Tony Cooke courtesy Colour-Rail.

Below PONTOP CROSSING – NO. 65865

Worsdell J27 no. 65865 passes Pontop Crossing signal box on 28th September 1962. The locomotive was Sunderland-allocated at the time. Photograph by Tony Cooke courtesy Colour-Rail.

Above REEDSMOUTH STATION – NO. 65857
Freight is shunted at Reedsmouth station (north of Hexham) by Worsdell J27 no. 65857 in the early 1960s. Photograph by John Arnott-Brown courtesy A1 Steam Trust.

Below REDMARSHALL – NO. 63380
Near Stockton-on-Tees, a dolomite train passes Redmarshall East signal box on 4th June 1961 behind Raven Q6 no. 63380. Photograph by David P. Williams courtesy Rail-Online.

Above SEAHAM HARBOUR

Lewin 0-4-0ST no. 18 was constructed in Dorset during 1877 to work at Seaham harbour, south of Sunderland. This continued to 1969 and the engine was subsequently preserved at the Beamish Museum. No. 18 is still employed on the harbour lines here on 7th July 1967. Photograph by Peter Fitton courtesy Rail Photoprints.

Below SEAHAM – NO. 63395

Carrying a particularly damaged snow plough at Seaham on 4th February 1967 is Raven Q6 no. 63395. Withdrawal occurred in September. Photograph by Ray Oakley courtesy Colour-Rail.

Above SHILDON – NO. 77002

A loaded train of coal wagons emerges from the southern portal of Shildon tunnel behind BR Standard Class 3 2-6-0 no. 77002 on 14th June 1962. The tunnel was built in the early 1840s as the Stockton & Darlington line was extended towards Bishop Auckland. The south portal is currently Grade II listed. No. 77002 was a West Auckland engine at the time and moved on to Darlington at the end of the year. Photograph courtesy Rail-Online.

Above SLEEKBURN – NO. 65789

North of Blyth, Worsdell J27 no. 65789 has a train of coal wagons at Sleekburn on 11th January 1965. Photograph by Geoff Warnes.

Opposite below SHILDON – NO. 60004

The Darlington to Newcastle via Bishop Auckland portion of the 'Blyth and Tyne' railtour is at Shildon with Gresley A4 Pacific no. 60004 *William Whitelaw* on 19th September 1965. The locomotive was the main motive power for the day, which began and ended at Leeds, with support provided by Ivatt 4MT no. 43057. Photograph by Hugh Ballantyne courtesy Rail Photoprints.

Below SLEEKBURN – NO. 65834

An unusually well-presented J27, no. 65834, is working at Sleekburn on 11th January 1965. Photograph by Geoff Warnes.

SOUTH PELAW – NO. 63760
A Tyne Dock-Consett iron ore train passes through South Pelaw with Thompson O1 no. 63760 in the mid-1950s. Photograph from the Dave Cobbe Collection courtesy Rail Photoprints.

Above SLEEKBURN – NO. 65874

J27 no. 65874 briefly holds traffic at a level crossing near Sleekburn on 11th January 1965. The engine was condemned at North Blyth shed in August 1966. Photograph by Geoff Warnes.

Below SOUTH PELAW – NO. 92064

Coal bound for the steel works at Consett is at South Pelaw (near Chester-le-Street) with BR 9F no. 92064 in July 1965. The engine had a spell in the Midlands at Wellingborough and Toton before joining the ranks at Tyne Dock in mid-1956. Photograph from the Dave Cobbe Collection courtesy Rail Photoprints.

Above STOCKTON-ON-TEES STATION – NO. 90434

The Leeds Northern Railway reached Billingham in 1852 and one of the other stations on the line was at Stockton-on-Tees. This was in use until the early 1890s when rebuilt by the NER. The trainshed looks to be deteriorating in the background here and would continue to do so until the late 1970s when demolished. The present station – named just Stockton – is an extremely simplified facility on roughly the same site. A train of coal wagons is passing through the station area during 1967, led by WD 'Austerity' Class 2-8-0 no. 90434. Photograph courtesy Rail-Online.

Opposite above STOCKTON-ON-TEES STATION – NO. 60072

The early morning Sunderland to King's Cross train approaches Stockton-on-Tees station during the early to mid-1950s. The locomotive is Heaton-allocated Gresley A3 Class Pacific no. 60072 *Sunstar*. New to Gateshead in September 1924, the engine remained in the North East to June 1960 when a year's employment in Leeds began. Returning to Heaton in July 1961, no. 60072 was condemned there during October 1962. Photograph courtesy Rail-Online.

Opposite below SUNDERLAND, FULWELL – NO. 60839

North of Sunderland at Fulwell, Gresley V2 no. 60839 has an express on 8th June 1960. Built at Darlington in October 1938, the locomotive was one of thirty-nine ordered from the works in November 1936. As LNER no. 4810, York was allocated the engine when new and, apart from three months at Neville Hill in mid-1946, remained until condemned for scrap in October 1962. Photograph by D.J. Dippie.

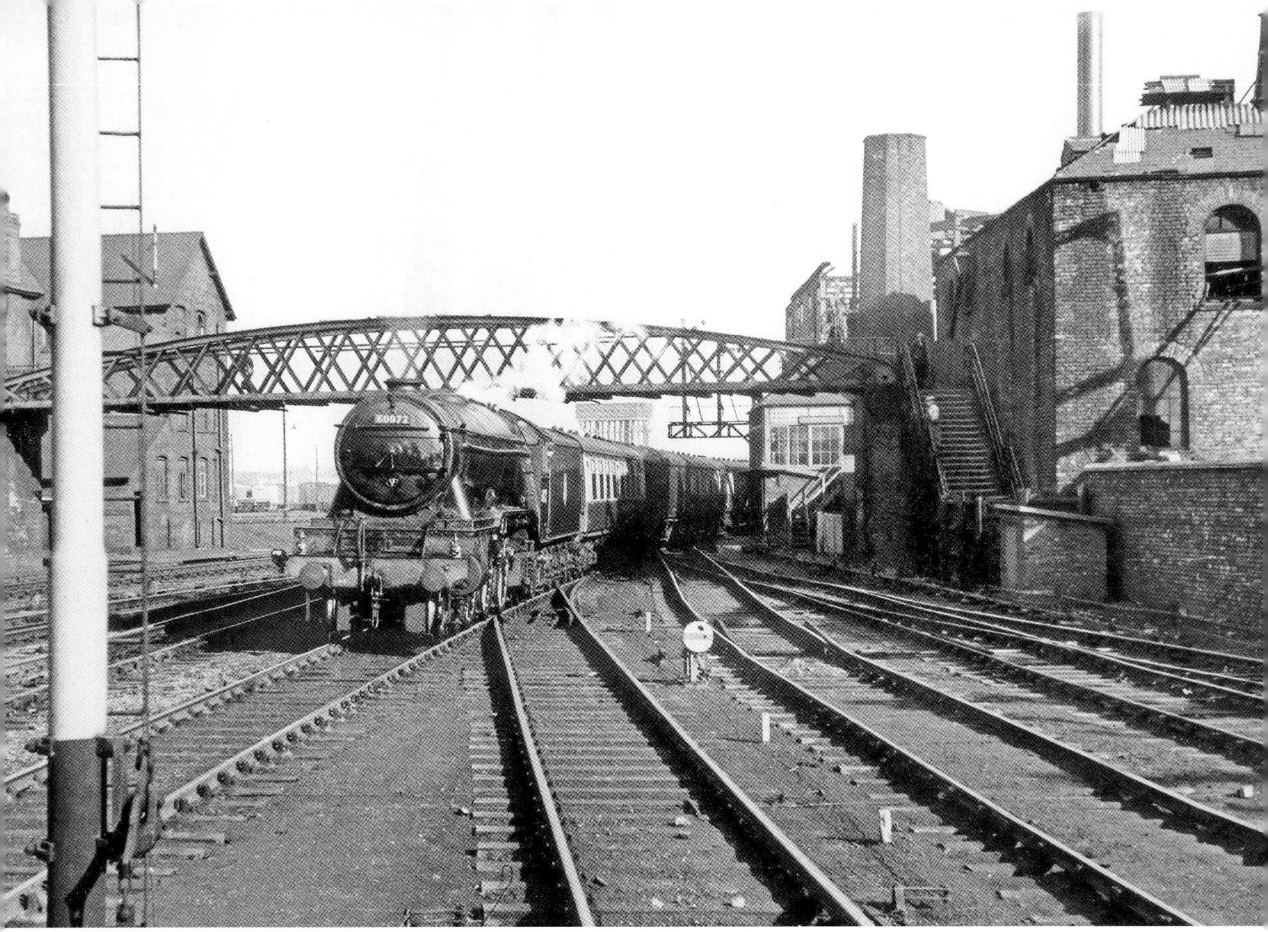
60072

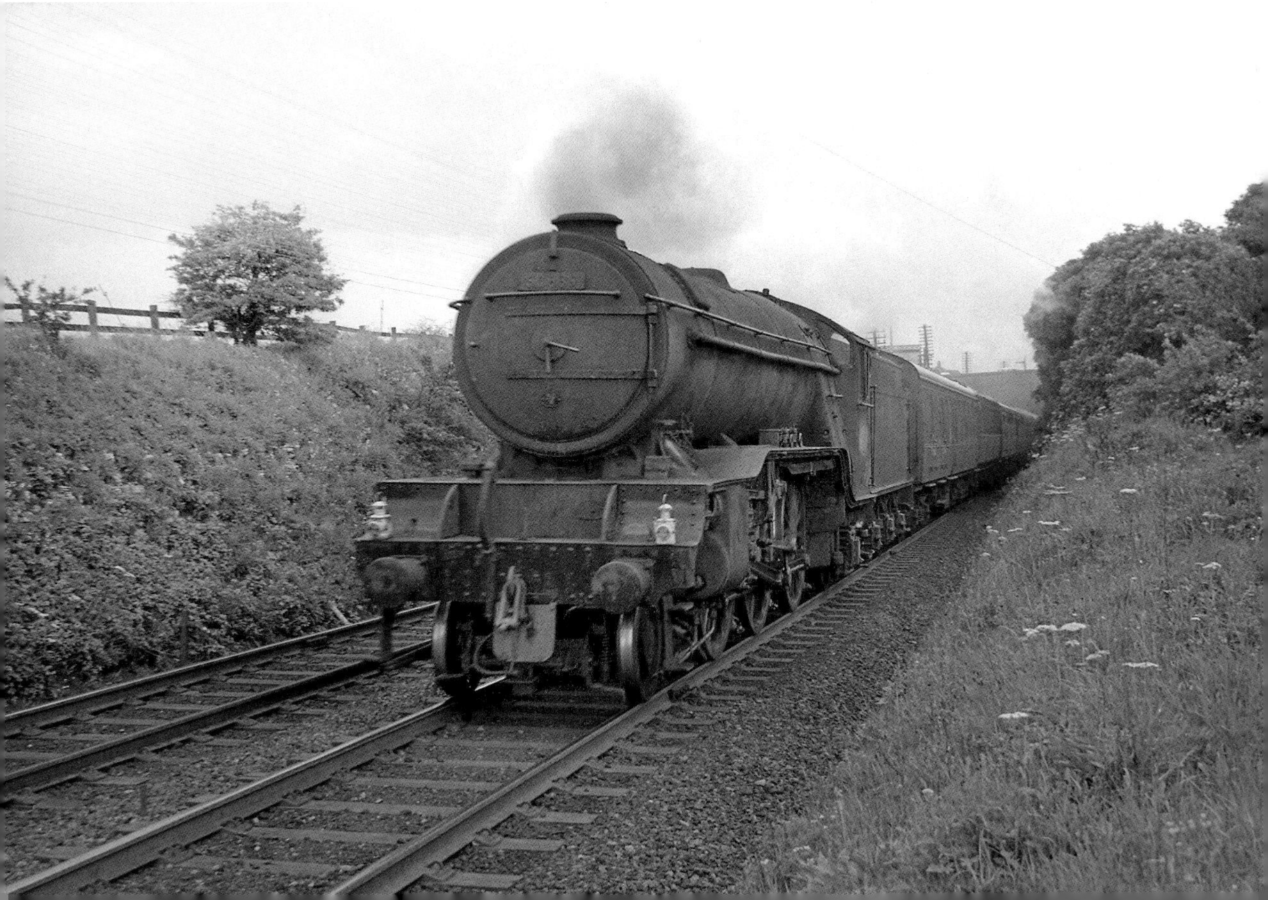

Below SUNDERLAND,
MONKWEARMOUTH – NO. 60074

In the late 1870s a project began to connect the railways on the north and south banks of the River Wear. Noted engineer T.E. Harrison designed the structure which had a length around 350 ft with a central span of 300 ft. Traffic across the bridge at Monkwearmouth began in 1879 and continues to the present, with the Metro now also using the crossing. Though a road bridge had been in use from the late 18th century, the structure seen here on the right was built in 1927. Gresley A3 no. 60074 *Harvester* has an express crossing the river here on 2nd February 1960. Photograph by D.J. Dippie.

Above SUNDERLAND, MONKWEARMOUTH – NO. 60065

Towards the end of 1923, the LNER placed orders for more Gresley A1s, with Doncaster receiving a request for 20 and the remainder sent to the North British Locomotive Company's Hyde Park Works, Glasgow. No. 2564 *Knight of the Thistle* was the second of the order constructed at the latter in July 1924 and was allocated new to Haymarket shed. The name was changed to *Knight of Thistle* for an unknown reason in December 1932; the latter was carried to the end of the locomotive's career. Under BR, no. 60065 moved to England and was mainly at Grantham, this covering the period September 1951 to June 1962. The engine is pictured with an express on Monkwearmouth bridge on 28th February 1960. Photograph by D.J. Dippie.

SUNDERLAND, PORTOBELLO LANE – NO. 60060

A goods train is prepared for departure at Portobello Lane sidings, Sunderland, on 29th June 1962. Gresley A3 no. 60060 *The Tetrarch* is the locomotive. Photograph by D.J. Dippie.

Above SUNDERLAND, MONKWEARMOUTH STATION – NO. 60112

One of four A3s fitted with small 'wing-type' smoke deflectors in the late 1950s was no. 60112 *St Simon*. The engine has an express at Monkwearmouth station on 13th March 1960. Photograph by D.J. Dippie.

Below SUNDERLAND, MONKWEARMOUTH STATION – NO. 60856

Gresley V2 no. 60856 passes Gresley J39 Class no. 64936, which appears to have a permanent way train, at Monkwearmouth station on 18th May 1961. Photograph by D.J. Dippie.

SUNDERLAND, RYHOPE GRANGE JUNCTION – NO. 63395

Just south of Sunderland, Q6 no. 63395 has a train of empty coal wagons at Ryhope Grange Junction during August 1965. Photograph courtesy Rail-Online.

SUNDERLAND SHED

A trio of Worsdell J27 locomotives – no. 65878, no. 65850 and 65871 – as well as a trio of J94 Class 0-6-0ST shunting engines – no. 68016, no. 68041 and no. 68044 – are stabled inside Sunderland shed on 26th March 1961. Photograph by D.J. Dippie.

Above SUNDERLAND, RYHOPE GRANGE JUNCTION – NO. 65854

The line between Hartlepool and Sunderland split before reaching the latter at Ryhope Grange Junction, with one line going to the docks and the other to Sunderland station. A train of coal wagons is near the junction with J27 no. 65854 on 29th February 1960. Photograph by D.J. Dippie.

Below SUNDERLAND, RYHOPE GRANGE JUNCTION – NO. 64703

Sunderland shed's J39 Class no. 64703 has a mineral train at Ryhope Grange Junction on 29th February 1960. The locomotive was allocated there from December 1959 to March 1962 when condemned. Photograph by D.J. Dippie.

Above SUNDERLAND, SEABURN STATION – NO. 60877

Seaburn station, north of Monkwearmouth, was a late addition to the line between Sunderland and Newcastle, being opened on 3rd May 1937 by the LNER. Along with several others on the route, the station was transferred to the Tyne & Wear Metro in the early 2000s. Gresley V2 Class no. 60877 is running through the station an express on 12th June 1960. Six months earlier, the locomotive transferred from Leeds to York and remained employed at the latter until withdrawn in February 1966. Photograph by D.J. Dippie.

SUNDERLAND SHED — NO. 64833 AND NO. 64854

Two withdrawn J19s linger on at Sunderland shed on 23rd May 1963. No. 64833 and no. 64854 left traffic at the end of 1962, though were not scrapped until late summer 1963. Photograph by D.J. Dippie

Above SUNDERLAND, SEAHAM JUNCTION – NO. 63455
At Seaham Junction, near Hendon Dock, Sunderland, Q6 Class no. 63455 has a mineral train in the mid-1960s. Photograph courtesy Rail-Online.

Below SUNDERLAND SHED – NO. 64701
Around 1960, Gresley J39 Class no. 64701 is at Sunderland shed. The engine worked in the North East from new in 1926, spending time at several locations. No. 64701 was at Sunderland from December 1959 to November 1962. Photograph by D.J. Dippie.

SUNDERLAND SHED – NO. 65835

J27 no. 65835 is seen from Sunderland shed yard on 23rd May 1963. Photograph by D.J. Dippie.

Above SUNDERLAND SHED
A pair of Gresley V3s and a V1 2-6-2T are at Sunderland shed on 8th October 1961. At the rear is no. 67642, in the middle stands no. 67683 and right is no. 67639. Photograph by D.J. Dippie.

Below SUNDERLAND SHED – NO. 62026
Arriving at Sunderland shed from Gateshead in February 1965, Peppercorn K1 no. 62026 is in the yard a few months later on 19th July. The engine moved on to Tyne Dock in October 1966. Photograph by Bill Wright.

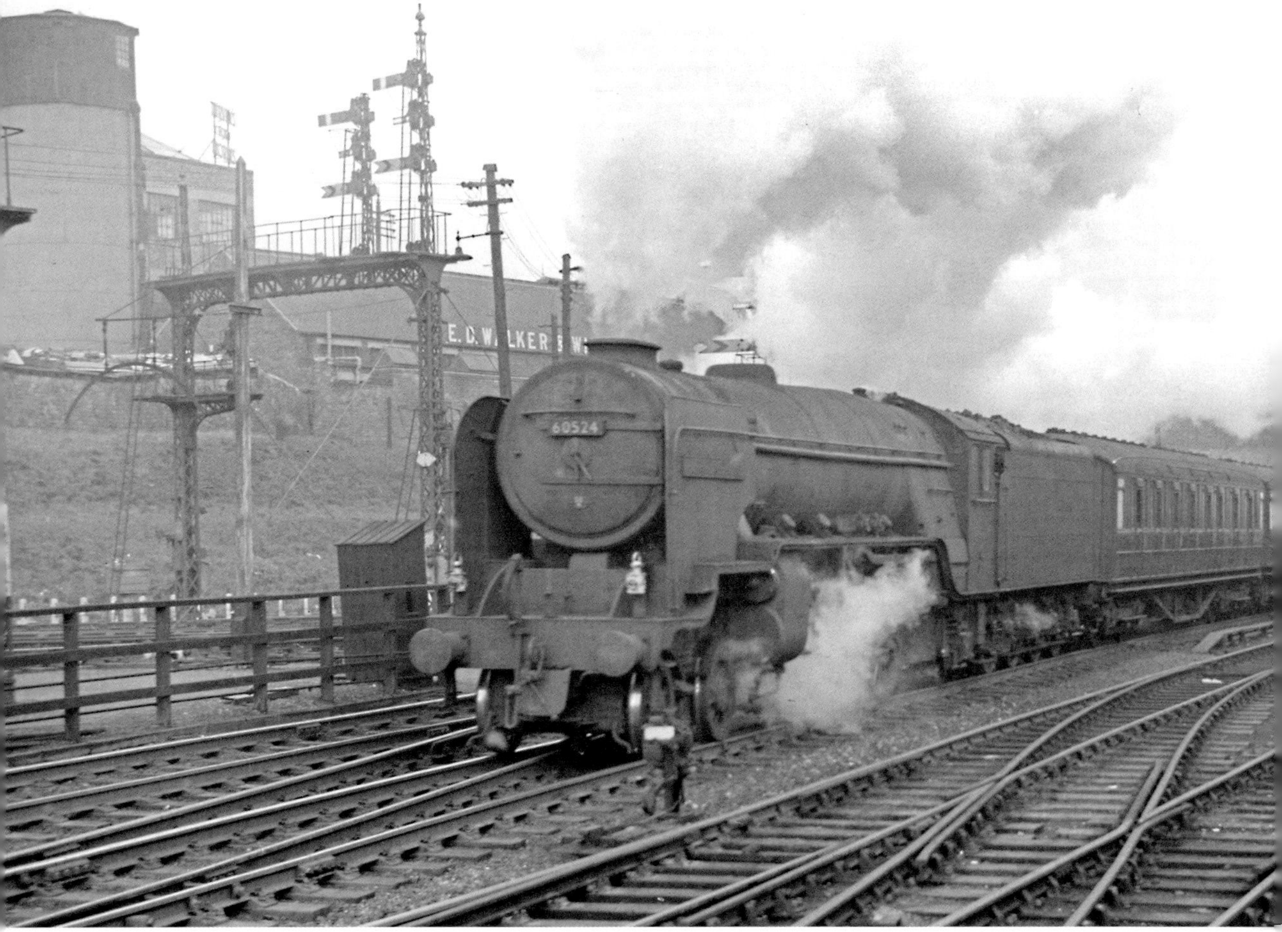
E. C. WALKER
60524

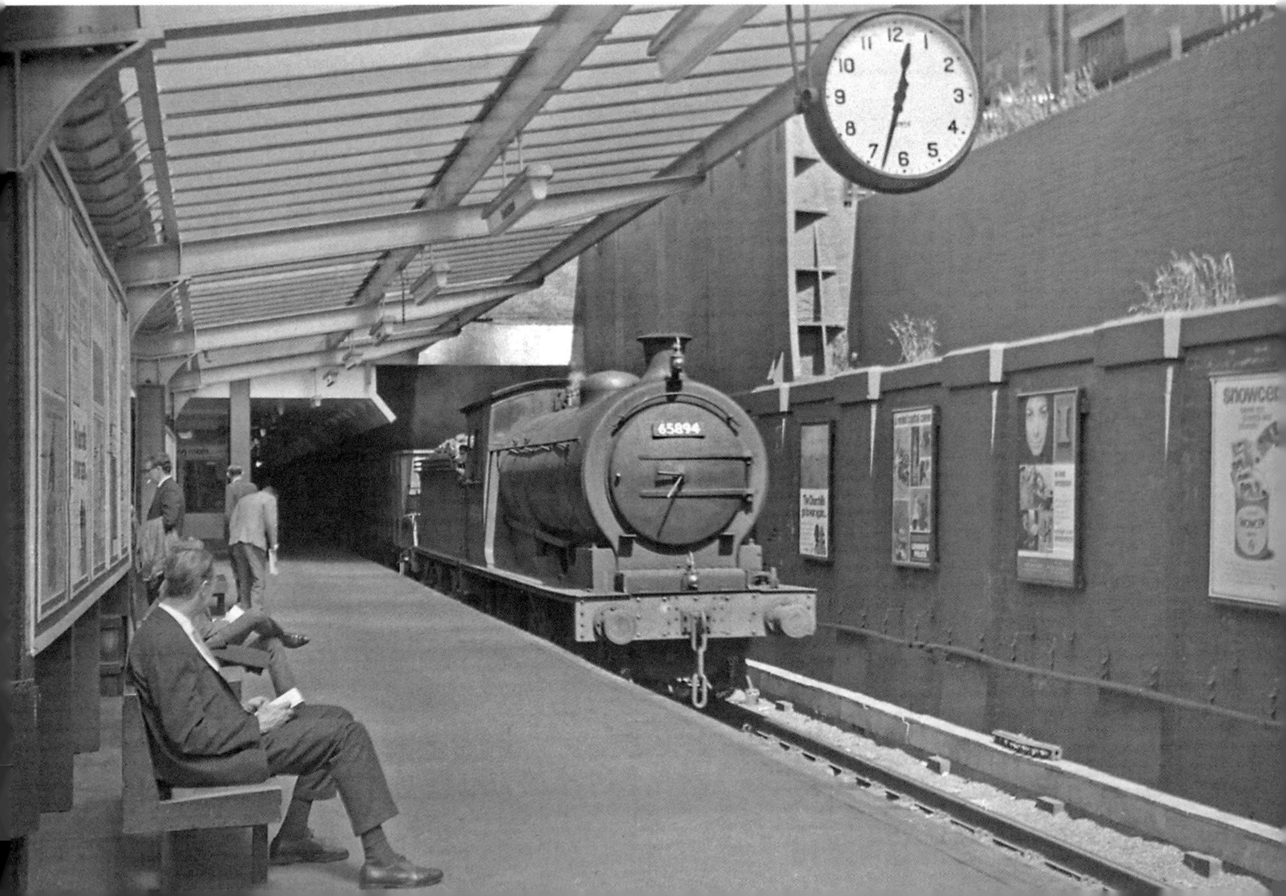
65894

Opposite above SUNDERLAND CENTRAL STATION –
NO. 60524

The first station in Sunderland dated from 1836 when Moor station opened near the docks on the Sunderland & Durham Railway line from Hetton-le-Hole. Fawcett Street station began serving passengers from 1853 when a line from Penshaw opened under the York, Newcastle & Berwick Railway. A route from Seaham arrived in the mid-1850s and Hendon Burn station was provided for travellers. With several stations around the local area in the 1870s, the NER decided to centralise services at Sunderland and opened a new station in August 1879. Thompson A2/3 no. 60524 *Herringbone* is seen departing from the south end on 6th March 1960. Photograph by D.J. Dippie.

Opposite below SUNDERLAND CENTRAL STATION –
NO. 65894

In July 1967, a coal train passes through Sunderland Central station with J27 Class no. 65894. The locomotive survived for another two months before condemned at Sunderland depot. The early 1960s saw the complete renovation of the station and the surrounding area which was completed in 1965. From opening to 1969, the station was known as Sunderland Central. Photograph by John Atkinson courtesy Rail-Online.

Below SUNDERLAND, VILLETTE ROAD – NO. 60053
South of Sunderland Central, Gresley A3 no. 60053 *Sansovino* has an express passing Villette Road signal box on 20th March 1960. Photograph by D.J. Dippie.

TEES YARD – NO. 90116
At Tees Yard with a mixed freight on 17th April 1967 is 'Austerity' Class 2-8-0 no. 90116. Photograph by Bill Wright.

Above **TEES YARD – NO. 63397**
Q6 no. 63397 has arrived at Tees Yard with a local freight train on 17th April 1967. Withdrawal from West Hartlepool occurred in late May. Photograph by Bill Wright.

Below **THORNABY – NO. 90309**
Another West Hartlepool engine is on Teesside during mid-April 1967 – 'Austerity' no. 90309 has coal wagons at Thornaby. Photograph by Bill Wright.

TEES YARD — NO. 90116

No. 90116 is seen again in Tees Yard on the same day with a load coal train. Photograph by Bill Wright.

Above THORNABY STATION – NO. 43100
Tender-first through Thornaby station on 5th November 1966, Ivatt 4MT no. 43100 has a freight train featuring trestle wagons loaded with steel plate. Photograph by Chris Davies courtesy Rail Photoprints.

Below THORNABY STATION – NO. 63397
A DMU is at the platform with a local service, while Q6 no. 63397 has a freight train at Thornaby station on 17th April 1967. Photograph by Bill Wright.

THORNABY SHED – NO. 60010
Gresley A4 no. 60010 *Dominion of Canada*
is at Thornaby shed for servicing on 14th
May 1960. Photograph by D.J. Dippie.

TYNE DOCK – NO. 65728
A freight train is running behind J25 Class no. 65728 at Tyne Dock on 8th April 1961. Photograph by D.J. Dippie.

TYNE DOCK – NO. 63377
Raven Q6 no. 63377 looks to be shunting these hopper wagons at Tyne Dock on 14th July 1966. Photograph courtesy Rail-Online.

Above TYNE DOCK – NO. 92061
Reversing away from Tyne Dock shed, BR 9F no. 92061 is ready to take up another train on 14th July 1966. The engine survived for another two months. Photograph courtesy Rail-Online.

Below TYNE DOCK SHED – NO. 92099
Several different types of tender were built for the 9Fs and these catered to particular requirements of the operating regions. Those for the North Eastern Region had water pick-up apparatus omitted and possessed a water capacity of 4,725 gallons, with space for 7 tons of coal. No. 92099 is fuelled at Tyne Dock shed's coal stage on 14th July 1966. Photograph courtesy Rail-Online.

Above **TYNE DOCK – NO. 63409**

An iron ore train begins the 26-mile journey from Tyne Dock to Consett on 14th July 1966. BR 9F no. 92061 is at the head whilst assistance from the rear is provided by Raven Q6 no. 63409. The latter was allocated to Tyne Dock shed from December 1962 until November 1966 and the engine went on to be scrapped in Hull where, as NER no. 2252, Darlington sent the locomotive when new just over 47 years earlier. Tyne Dock signal box is seen on the right. Photograph courtesy Rail-Online.

Opposite **TYNE DOCK**

A view over Tyne Dock from 21st May 1960. Even before the industrial revolution, the River Tyne was an important departure point for goods produced in the local area, as well as receiving goods from overseas. From the 17th century, the traffic to the Tyne was mostly coal, whilst an import related to this was timber for mining supports. Several areas along the Tyne were developed for dock activities and Tyne Dock was built in the late 1850s on the south bank to the east of Jarrow. The site continues in use at present, though exports are now mainly locally produced cars and coal is imported. In this scene, a train of steel products is banked in the yard. Photograph courtesy Rail-Online.

TYNE DOCK SHED – NO. 63455

Raven Q6 no. 63455 stands in the shell of a roundhouse at Tyne Dock shed in May 1965. Photograph from the Gordon Edgar Collection courtesy Rail Photoprints.

Above TYNE DOCK SHED – NO. 62005
A mechanical issue is preventing Peppercorn K1 no. 62005 from being turned quickly at Tyne Dock shed on 13th September 1967. A few days earlier, the locomotive was briefly involved in a railtour which likely accounts for exterior appearance at this time. Photograph courtesy Rail Photoprints.

Below TYNE DOCK SHED – NO. 63460
A three-cylinder version of Raven's successful Q6 was introduced just before Grouping. Just five Q7s (NER T3 Class) were built initially, though the LNER added a further ten. No. 63460 was one of the original engines built at Darlington in 1919 and is seen here at Tyne Dock shed on 4th October 1961. Photograph by D.J. Dippie.

Opposite above TYNE DOCK SHED – NO. 63350

A freight train from Tyne Dock passes the engine shed behind Q6 no. 63350 on 3rd February 1962. Under BR, the engine arrived at the depot from Borough Gardens in June 1959 and was employed to withdrawal in June 1963. Photograph by D.J. Dippie.

Opposite below TYNE DOCK SHED – NO. 63464

The introduction of Raven's Q7 appears to have been an experiment into the advantages and disadvantages of three-cylinder propulsion. In the North East, the traffic was suitably provided for with existing types leaving the Q7s operating within their means. In the 1940s, the class was concentrated at Tyne Dock shed to work the iron ore trains and this remained their main task until the 9Fs arrived in the mid-1950s. No. 63464 was displaced at this time to Blaydon, then Sunderland before returning to Tyne Dock for the last three years in traffic. The engine is on the depot's turntable on 3rd June 1961. Photograph by D.J. Dippie.

Below TYNE DOCK SHED

A group of locomotives are inside one of the roundhouses at Tyne Dock shed on 22nd May 1961. Two J94s are on the left, no. 68031 and no. 68036, and to the right are a pair of Worsdell J25s, no. 65663 and no. 65670. Three roundhouses were built in the late 19th century and were in use until September 1967, subsequently being demolished. Photograph by D.J. Dippie.

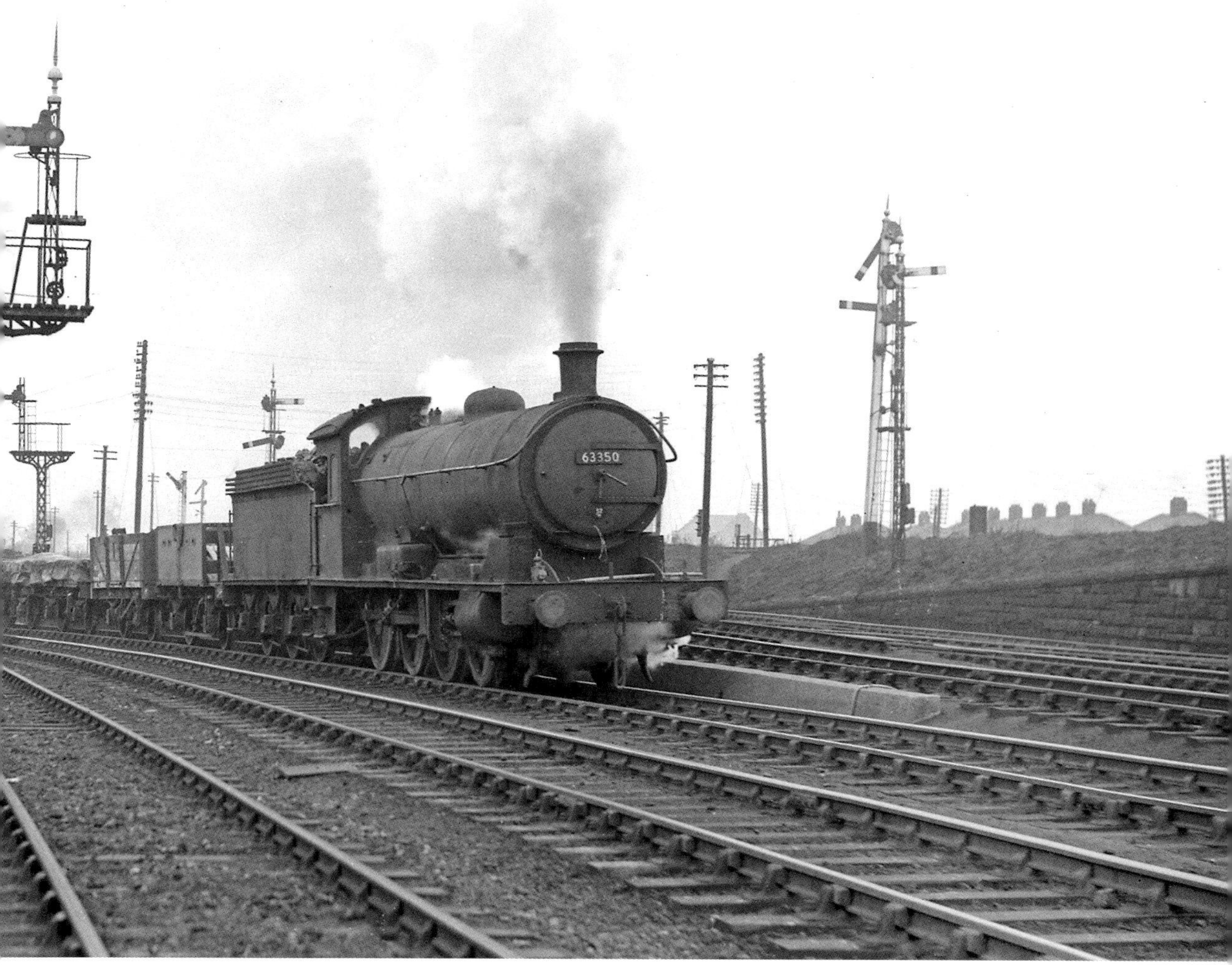
63350

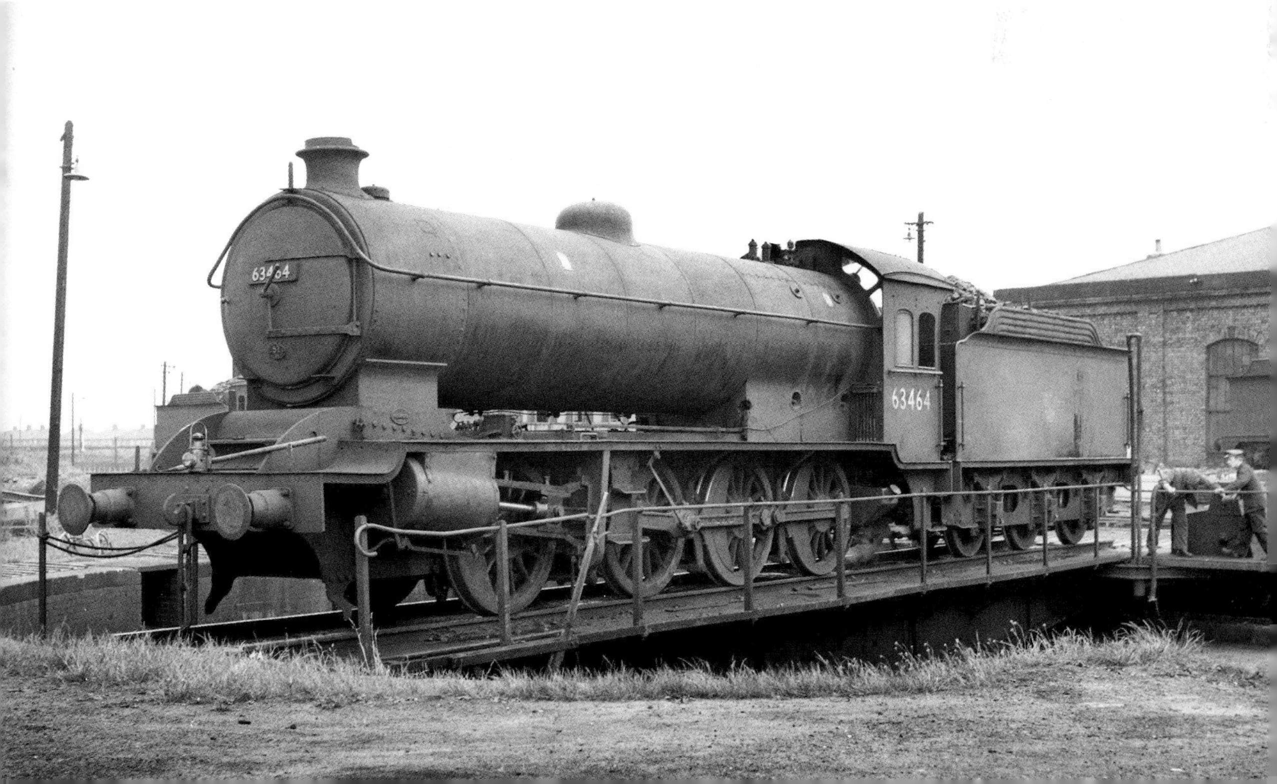
63464
63464

TYNE DOCK SHED – NO. 65645
In the late 1950s, Worsdell J25 no. 65645 is on shed at Tyne Dock in the late 1950s. Photograph by John Arnott-Brown courtesy A1 Steam Trust.

Above TYNE DOCK SHED – NO. 68019

When purchased by the LNER, the J94 0-6-0ST shunters did not find a home initially at Tyne Dock shed. Later, class members worked at the depot, with no. 68019 there from May 1959 to October 1963. The engine is in the yard here on 22nd July 1961. Photograph by D.J. Dippie.

Below TYNE DOCK SHED – NO. 63460

Raven Q7 no. 63460 managed to weather the introduction of the 9Fs and remained at Tyne Dock from 1943 until condemned during December 1962. The engine is seen on 22nd May 1961. Photograph by D.J. Dippie.

Below WANSBECK VIADUCT – NO. 62017

The Blyth & Tyne Railway gradually expanded from early wooden wagonways feeding coal from the pits to the Tyne to a larger operation connecting much of the area from the Tyne to the Wansbeck river. In the late 1850s, the route was built from Bedlington to Morpeth and shortly afterwards an extension from Bedlington to North Seaton was laid. This latter crossed the River Wansbeck on a wooden viaduct 400 yards in length which was reputedly the greatest wooden structure in Britain at the time. By the 1920s this required replacement and a steel trestle bridge with 14 spans carrying the line 86 ft above the river's surface was standing before the end of the decade. Here, on 1st June 1966, Peppercorn K1 no. 62017 has a coal train for Cambois Power Station. Photograph by Hugh Ballantyne courtesy Rail Photoprints.

Above WASHINGTON STATION – NO. 63364

The first station at Washington was opened by the Stanhope & Tyne Railway. This line was developed to transport limestone and coal to South Shields and had been running trains from September 1834, being reluctant to engage in passenger service. Public demand soon saw this change, however, as in mid-April 1835 the conveyance of people began, though initially on top of coal before a dedicated wagon was provided. As the railways in the area developed, improved connections were deemed desirable and a deviation from the original route from the south (Darlington and Durham) to Gateshead and Newcastle was made in 1850. This resulted in a new station being built at Washington and the line was the main East Coast route until diverted via Durham in the early 1870s. As a result, the section through Washington developed a concentration of freight services and the station itself was a hub for local traffic with extensive sidings and a chemical works located adjacent (here on the right). With the rundown of both passenger and freight generally in the 1950s and 1960s, Washington station closed completely in 1964 and recently the route has been lifted. A train of hopper wagons is at Washington with Raven Q6 no. 63364, c. 1960. Photograph by Philip Jackson courtesy A1 Steam Trust.

WEST HARTLEPOOL – NO. 63440

Running through West Hartlepool on 31st May 1966 is Q6 no. 63440. The locomotive was in service for another six months. Photograph by M. Beckett courtesy Colour-Rail

Above WEARHEAD STATION – NO. 65078
The last train on the Weardale branch is about to depart from Wearhead station on 27th June 1953. Worsdell J21 0-6-0 no. 65078 has the service. Photograph by B.W.L. Brooksbank.

Below WEST HARTLEPOOL – NO. 60539
A diverted express passes through West Hartlepool with Peppercorn A2 Pacific no. 60539 *Bronzino* in 1960. Photograph from the Norman Preedy Archive courtesy Rail Photoprints.

Above WEST HARTLEPOOL SHED – NO. 63438
A few days after returning to traffic following a general repair at Darlington in September 1957, Q6 no. 63438 awaits the next duty at West Hartlepool shed. Photograph courtesy Rail Photoprints.

Below WEST HARTLEPOOL SHED – NO. 68233
Built at Darlington Works in February 1887, Worsdell J71 Class 0-6-0T no. 68233 was 67 years old when caught working near West Hartlepool shed on 13th June 1954. The locomotive's career continued until February 1961. Photograph by B.W.L. Brooksbank.

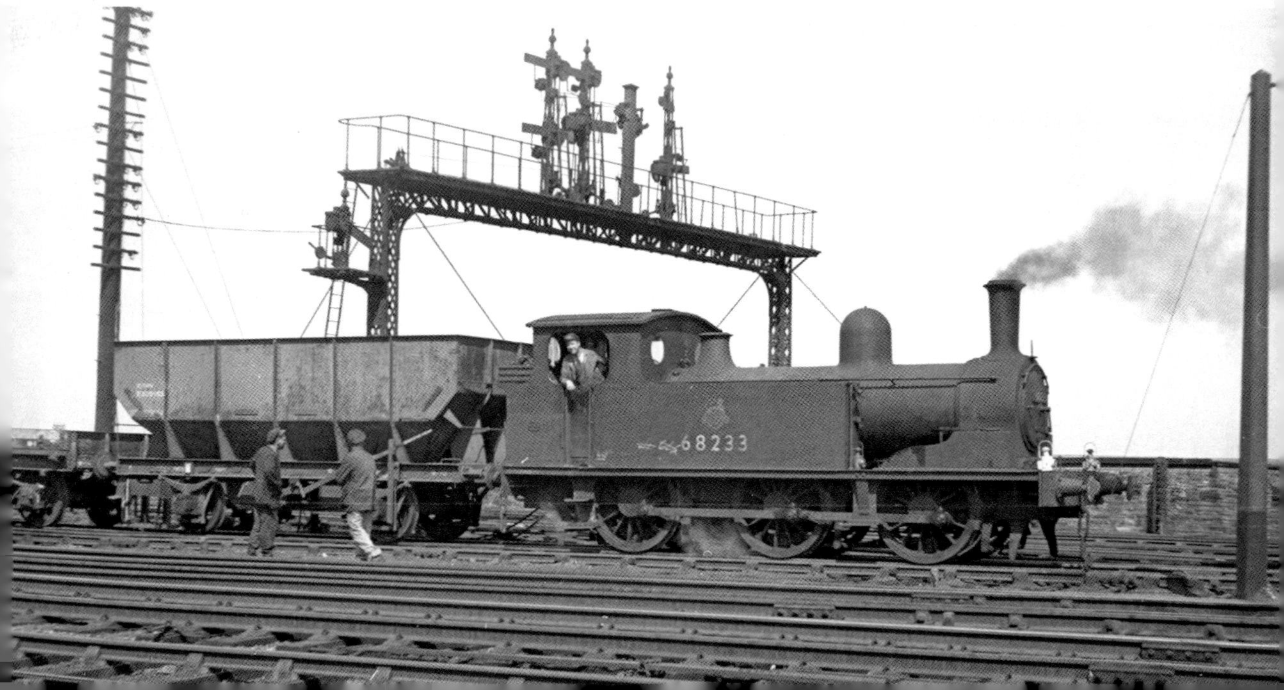

Above WEST HARTLEPOOL – NO. 63421
A train of timber loaded into open wagons is seen at West Hartlepool in 1965 with locally-based Raven Q6 no. 63421. A long-term servant at the depot, the locomotive arrived in 1945 and remained to withdrawal in June 1966. Photograph courtesy Rail-Online.

Below WEST HARTLEPOOL – NO. 62044
With the ramp for the coal stage at West Hartlepool shed in the background, no. 62044 travels by with a coal train in mid-September 1966. Photograph by David Christie.

WEST HARTLEPOOL SHED
A diesel locomotive intrudes on this scene captured at West Hartlepool shed in August 1967. Photograph courtesy Rail Photoprints.

Above WEST HARTLEPOOL SHED – NO. 45562

The 'North Eastern No. 3' railtour has brought Stanier 'Jubilee' Class 4-6-0 no. 45562 *Alberta* to West Hartlepool shed on 6th May 1967. Photograph by Chris Davies courtesy Rail Photoprints.

Below WEST HARTLEPOOL STATION – NO. 90348

West Hartlepool station dates from 1880 when replacing an earlier facility opened by the Stockton & Hartlepool Railway in 1841. In 1967 the station's name was changed to Hartlepool. 'Austerity' no. 90348 has a coal train here just before the switch occurred. Photograph courtesy Rail-Online.

Opposite above WEST SLEEKBURN – NO. 43012

Passing Winning signal box at West Sleekburn is a coal train hauled by Ivatt 4MT no. 43012. The box controlled the curve eastward from the Bedlington-Ashington line to the Cambois branch, as well as a level crossing which has traffic stopped here. This image dates from 28th March 1967 when no. 43012 was working from North Blyth shed. The engine transferred from the London Midland Region at Heaton Mersey in August 1966. Photograph courtesy Rail-Online.

Opposite below WEST SLEEKBURN – NO. 62024

Also on the Cambois branch at West Sleekburn is Peppercorn K1 no. 62024, though seen earlier on 2nd August 1966. New from the North British Locomotive Company in August 1949, no. 62024 was in the North East until condemned in February 1967, mainly at Blaydon, though in the 1960s was at Gateshead then North Blyth depots. Photograph courtesy Colour-Rail.

Below WEST SLEEKBURN – NO. 65860

The line between Bedlington and Ashington passed through West Sleekburn on the south bank of the River Wansbeck. A junction was made there with the branch to Cambois. A train of 'Esso' branded oil tankers is at West Sleekburn on 2nd August 1966 with Worsdell J27 no. 65860. Served by the line were two collieries, West Sleekburn and Bomarsund, with the two headgears of the latter visible here behind the train. Photograph courtesy Colour-Rail.

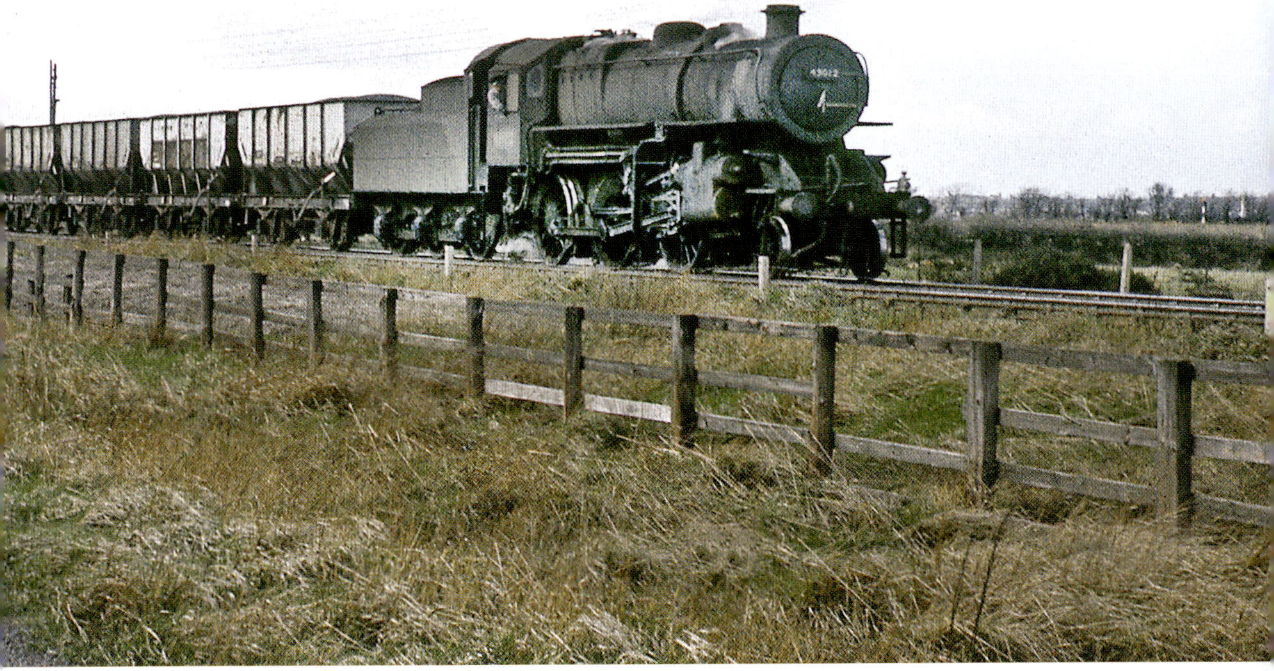

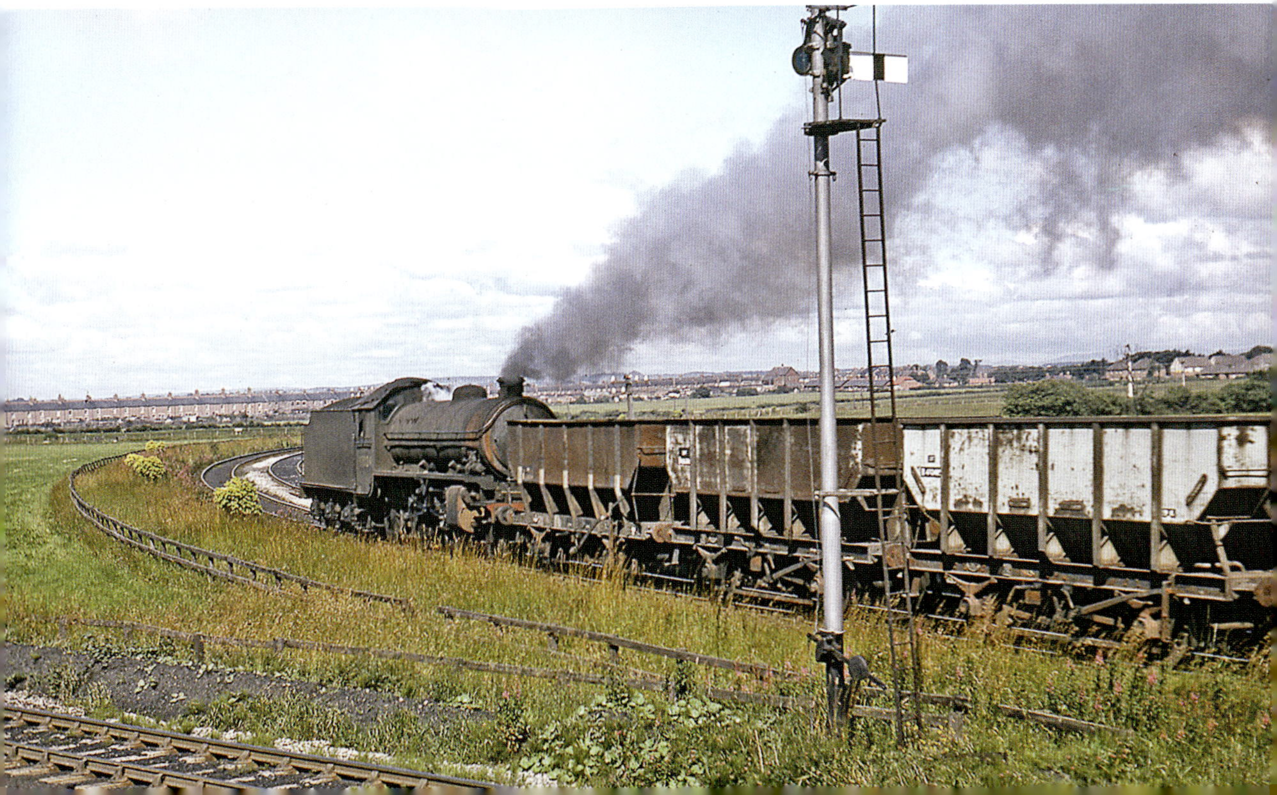

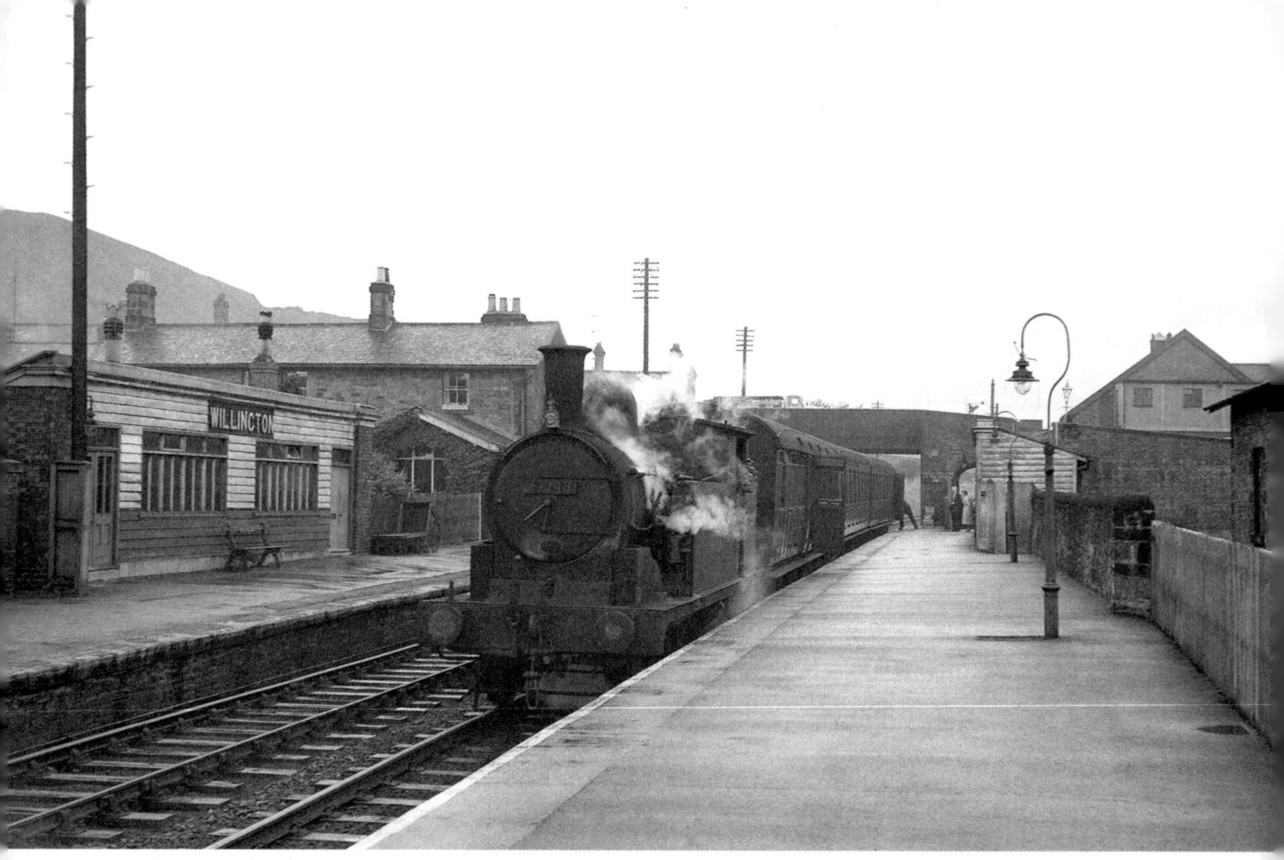
WILLINGTON

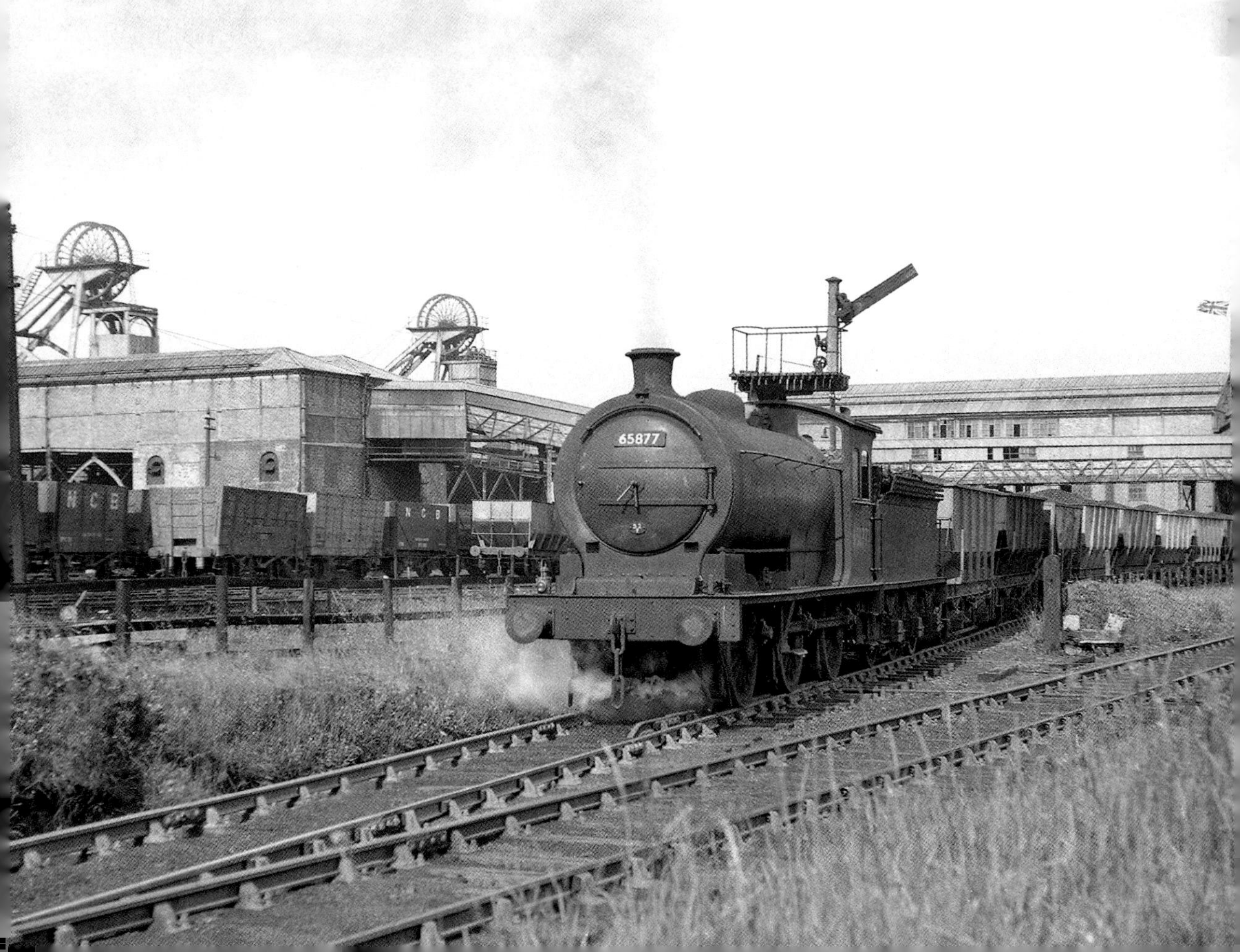
65877
N C B
N C B

Above WOODBURN STATION – NO. 65834

Following the development of railways in the area – the line from Newcastle to Berwick and Hexham to Riccarton Junction – a new route between Morpeth and Reedsmouth was proposed in the late 1850s. The Wansbeck Railway was approved in 1859 and construction began soon after, being completed in stages. The final part was ready in 1865. Woodburn station was the second from Reedsmouth and opened at the latter date. The line mainly served locals, with little industrial traffic, resulting in the end of passenger trains in 1952 and freight in October 1966. A weekly goods service is at Woodburn station here on 2nd June 1966 and Worsdell J27 no. 65834 is shunting wagons into sidings. Photograph by Hugh Ballantyne courtesy Rail Photoprints.

Opposite above WILLINGTON STATION – NO. 67248

Edward Fletcher broke the NER's use of old tender engines for local passenger trains in the early 1870s with the 'Bogie Tank Passenger' or 'BTP' 0-4-4T design. In the mid-1890s Fletcher's successor Wilson Worsdell modified the type to produce the O Class and over seven years one hundred and ten were built at Darlington. The main differences between the 'BTP' and O Classes saw the coupled wheel diameter reduced and fuel/water capacities increased. No. 67248 was amongst the first ten from Darlington in 1894 as NER no. 1769. Here, the locomotive has a local train at Willington station on the Durham-Bishop Auckland line. Seen in 1957, the locomotive was Sunderland-allocated at the time. Willington station was also 100 years old during the year and remained in use for a further seven before closure. Photograph courtesy Rail-Online.

Opposite below WOODHORN COLLIERY – NO. 65877

To the east of Ashington, Woodhorn Colliery was established in 1894 and produced coal before the turn of the century. The site was active until 1966 when coal was brought to the surface at nearby Ashington Colliery. This event had yet to occur in this image at Woodhorn from the early 1960s. Worsdell J27 no. 65877 is ready to depart with a loaded coal train. The locomotive was taken out of service in October 1962. Woodhorn Colliery has subsequently become a museum and country park. Photograph courtesy Rail-Online.

BIBLIOGRAPHY

Allen, C.J. *The London & North Eastern Railway.* 1966.

Allen, C.J. *Titled Trains of Great Britain.* 1983.

Banks, Steve and Clive Carter. *LNER Passenger Trains and Formations 1923-1967: The Principal Services.* 2013.

Bolger, Paul. *BR Steam Motive Power Depots: North Eastern Region.* 2009.

British Rail Main Line Gradient Profiles.

Griffiths, Roger and Paul Smith. *The Directory of British Engine Sheds and Principal Locomotive Servicing Points: 2 North Midlands, Northern England and Scotland.* 2000.

Hoole, K. *A Regional History of the Railways of Great Britain Volume 4: The North East.* 1974.

Hoole, K. *North Eastern Locomotive Sheds.* 1972.

Hoole, K. *Rail Centres: Newcastle.* 2008.

Hooper, J. *The WD 'Austerity' 2-8-0: The BR Record.* 2010.

Quick, Michael. *Railway Passenger Stations in Great Britain: A Chronology.* 2009.

RCTS. *A Detailed History of British Railways Standard Steam Locomotives: Volume Two: The 4-6-0 and 2-6-0 Classes.* 2003.

RCTS. *A Detailed History of British Railways Standard Steam Locomotives: Volume Three: The Tank Engine Classes.* 2007.

RCTS. *A Detailed History of British Railways Standard Steam Locomotives: Volume Four: The 9F 2-10-0 Class.* 2008.

RCTS. *Locomotives of the LNER - Parts 1 to 10A.*

Rowland, Don. *British Railways Wagons.* 1985.

Steam for Scrap: The Complete Story.

Walmsley, Tony. *Shed by Shed Part Three: North Eastern.* 2010.

Yeadon, W.B. *Yeadon's Register of LNER Locomotives Volume One: Gresley A1 and A3 Classes.* 2001.

Yeadon, W.B. *Yeadon's Register of LNER Locomotives Volume Two: Gresley A4 and W1 Classes.* 2001.

Yeadon, W.B. *Yeadon's Register of LNER Locomotives Volume Three: Raven, Thompson & Peppercorn Pacifics.* 2001.

Yeadon, W.B. *Yeadon's Register of LNER Locomotives Volume Four: Gresley V2 and V4 Classes.* 2001.

Yeadon, W.B. *Yeadon's Register of LNER Locomotives Volume Six: Thompson B1.* 2001.

Yeadon, W.B. *Yeadon's Register of LNER Locomotives Volume Ten: Gresley D49 and J38 Classes.* 2001.

Yeadon, W.B. *Yeadon's Register of LNER Locomotives Volume Eighteen: Gresley K1 & K2, Thompson K1/1 & Peppercorn K1.* 2001.

Also available from Great Northern

The Last Years of Yorkshire Steam

The Golden Age of Yorkshire Railways

Gresley's A3s

Peppercorn's Pacifics

London Midland Steam 1948-1966

The Last Years of North East Steam

British Railways Standard Pacifics

Western Steam 1948-1966

The Last Years of North West Steam

Gresley's V2s

Southern Steam 1948-1967

Yorkshire Steam 1948-1967

Gresley's A4s

Gresley's B17s

The Last Years of West Midlands Steam

East Midlands Steam 1950-1966

Thompson's B1s

The Glorious Years of the LNER

Scottish Steam 1948-1967

The Last Years of London Steam

Gresley's D49s

visit www.*greatnorthernbooks.co.uk* for details.